THE MAPLE LEAF
FOREVER

THE MAPLE LEAF FOREVER

A CELEBRATION OF CANADIAN SYMBOLS

BY DONNA & NIGEL HUTCHINS

PHOTOGRAPHY BY MATTHEW BEVERLY

The BOSTON
MILLS PRESS

A Boston Mills Press Book

Copyright © 2006 Limestone Productions Ltd.

Library and Archives Canada Cataloguing in Publication

Hutchins, Donna Farron
        The maple leaf forever : a celebration of Canadian symbols / by
Donna & Nigel Hutchins ; Photography by Matthew Beverly (www.matty.ca).

Includes bibliographical references.
ISBN-13: 978-1-55046-474-0
ISBN-10: 1-55046-474-4

1. Emblems, National--Canada. 2. Signs and symbols--Canada.
3. Emblems, National--Canada--Pictorial works. 4. Signs and symbols--
Canada--Pictorial works. 5. Canada--Civilization. I. Hutchins, Nigel,
1945-
II. Beverly, Matthew III. Title.

CR212.H88 2006   971
C2006-901322-5

Publisher Cataloging-in-Publication Data (U.S.)

Hutchins, Donna Farron.
    The maple leaf forever : a celebration of Canadian symbols / by Donna & Nigel Hutchins ; Photography Matthew Beverly (www.matty.ca).
[224] p. : col. ill. ; cm.
Includes bibliographical references and index.
Summary: A collection of objects depicting Canada's three most enduring national symbols: the Mountie, the maple leaf and the beaver.
ISBN-13: 978-1-55046-474-0
ISBN-10: 1-55046-474-4
1. Emblems, National — Canada. 2. Signs and symbols — Canada.   I. Hutchins, Nigel, 1945- . II. Beverly, Matthew. III. Title.
971 dc22   CR212.H88 2006

Published by Boston Mills Press, 2006
132 Main Street, Erin, Ontario N0B 1T0
Tel: 519-833-2407 Fax: 519-833-2195
www.bostonmillspress.com

In Canada:
Distributed by Firefly Books Ltd.
66 Leek Crescent
Richmond Hill, Ontario, Canada L4B 1H1

In the United States:
Distributed by Firefly Books (U.S.) Inc.
P.O. Box 1338, Ellicott Station
Buffalo, New York 14205

The publisher gratefully acknowledges the financial support for our publishing program by Government of Canada through the Book Publishing Industry Development Program.

Concept by Donna Farron Hutchins
Project Design by Nigel Hutchins, S.D.S.A.
Art direction and layout by Matthew Beverly (www.matty.ca)

Printed in Singapore

All photography by Matthew Beverly (www.matty.ca) for Limestone Productions Ltd., except as follows:
P. 9   Mountie Quilt courtesy of the Canadian Museum of Civilization
P. 22,23,26,27   courtesy of HBC archives and The Beaver magazine
P. 93   courtesy of Canadian Pacific Railway archives
P.125   courtesy Whiz Bang Films Prod. Ltd.
P.126   courtesy of Chum Television (Chum Ltd.)
P.137   courtesy of Jeremie White
P.194   Table courtesy of Royal Ontario Museum
P.194   Gameboard courtesy of Waddingtons Auctioneers & Appraisers

Disclaimer
All reasonable efforts were made to acknowledge or trace ownership of copyrighted material. If an error or omission has occurred, the authors and publisher welcome new information that could be used in future editions.

The authors received no financial remuneration or funding from any corporation, individual or government agency. All items featured in the book appear as a result of their integral role in the graphic evolution of Canadian symbols.

Wherever possible, an actual or approximate date of production (e.g. circa 1820) has been specified for the objects herein. When date of production was unclear or unknown, items were dated to the nearest quarter century.

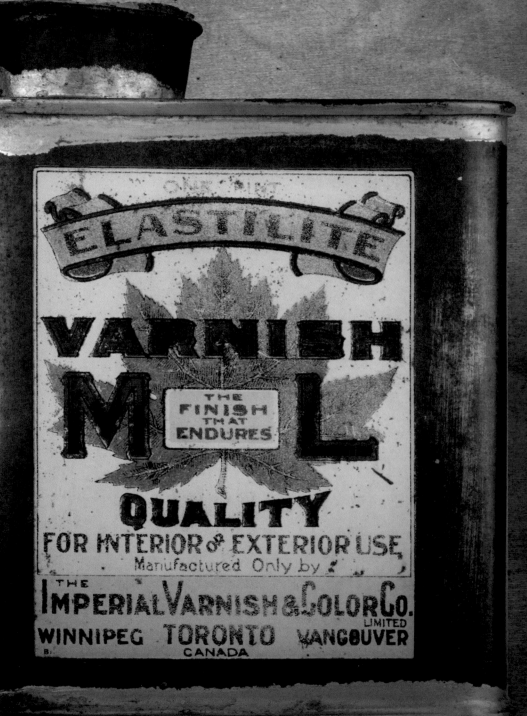

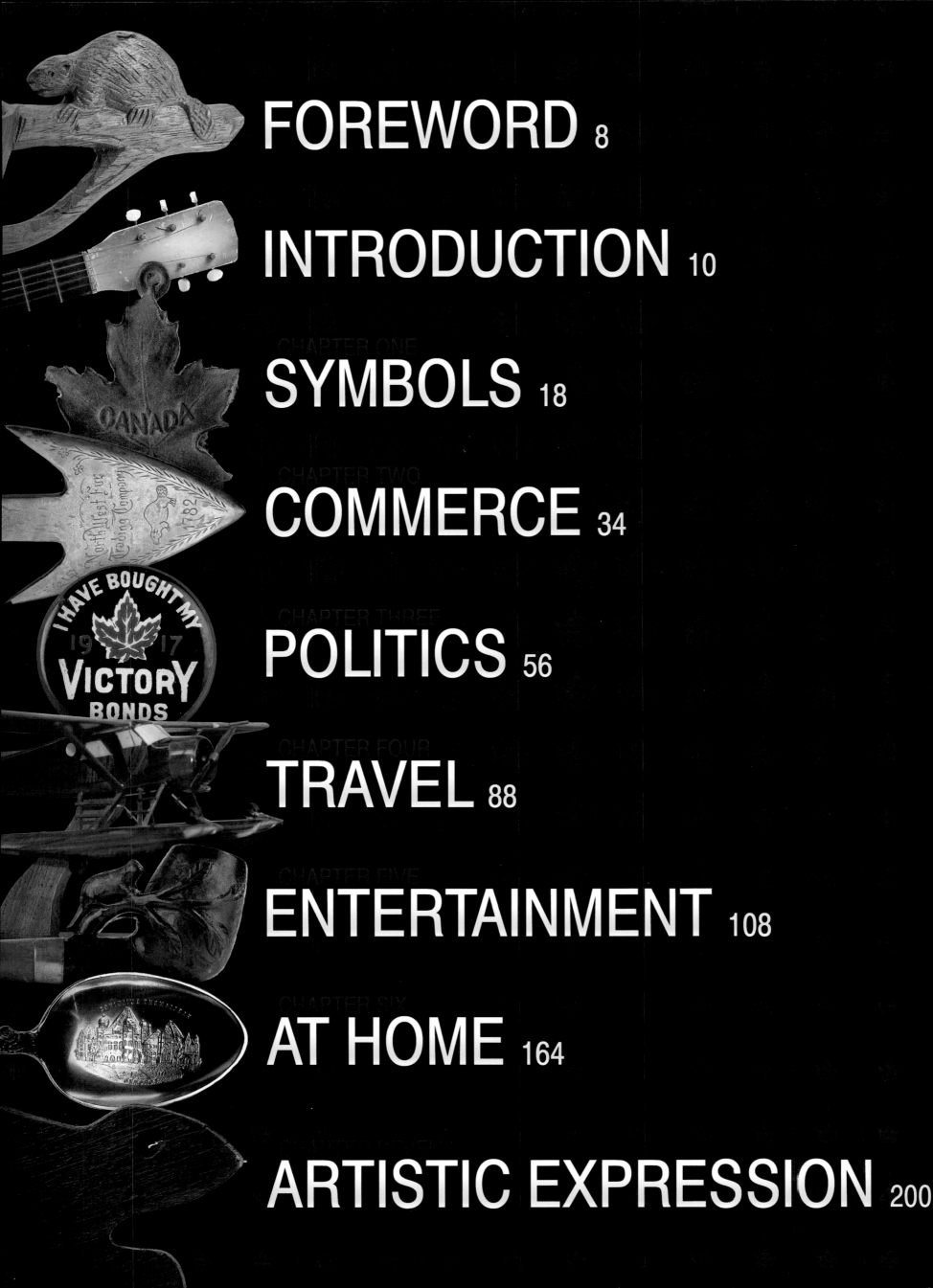

FOREWORD

The reader has a visual treat in store — and possibly a slight swelling of pride! On the following pages you will find pictured an amazing collection of objects depicting Canada's national symbols: Mountie, maple leaf and beaver. Although they fall into a broad grouping of categories, from art to icon to simple decoration, they are widely recognized as Canada's symbols. To borrow from the title of Russell Harper's wonderful book, these ubiquitous Canadian images are truly the "People's Art." Time has not diminished their popularity. They have a long history of use but are still seen everywhere today.

Common though the symbols may be, it is nonetheless remarkable that this book's wide-ranging collection could have been assembled. Included are items as varied as a centuries-old fishing spearhead, a goalie mask, war medals, a stove door, Easter eggs and comic books. The object types range from academic art through folk art to decorative and commercial art. The authors, of course, were not surprised by the scope of this subject when they began this project. Their own collection of this material has grown over several decades and accounts for the majority of objects pictured in this book. Donna and Nigel provide the reader with not only a feast of visual images, but also with a comprehensive history of the symbols and their use in Canada. In addition, they explore the subject of patriotism, candidly revealing their own patriotic feelings, set within the context of their respective national origins.

Symbols have been with us from man's beginning. They were especially important in pre-literate times. Abstract concepts were readily communicated through recognized symbols in art and religious icons. Practical, straightforward messages were also communicated by symbols in a variety of media. The carved or painted trade signs that guided the uneducated in earlier eras have now been succeeded by recognizable company logos that attract purchasers and, in some cases, loyal followers. Successful company logos and patriotic symbols trigger emotional responses often unrelated to their aesthetic content.

The message of patriotic symbols is one of meaning, power and commitment. Commitment is a motivating force that can be present in both the artist and the consumer of patriotic symbols. The continuing market for them proves that many consumers want to buy Canadian symbols.

This wooden canoe cup was hand-carved circa 1900. Utilitarian objects often became media for artistic expression. These cups, often carved from the burl of a tree, were used by the voyageurs.

The creation or use of patriotic symbols suggests allegiance and constancy. It shows an individual's commitment to the larger community, to the nation itself. It speaks of collective, communal memory, which is the binding agent of communities. In our homes we surround ourselves with images that support our impressions of the society that we live in, and Canadians often participate in the collective memory experience of their country by displaying its symbols, thereby celebrating their own identity and patriotism.

Patriotic symbols were of pressing interest to me in the 1970s and 1980s when I was responsible for developing the folk-art collections of the National Museum of Man in Ottawa. My colleagues and I noticed that some of the best, most powerful objects we collected had patriotic themes or symbols. In visiting folk artists in their homes across Canada, we regularly found that they possessed strong feelings for their country, which they expressed in their art. As the collecting, interviewing of artists and research continued, we began to see a pattern developing. It became clear that the most expressive and engaging pieces of art had been inspired by the artist's own strong emotions. The burning question for us always was, "What compelled them to do it?" By the time our efforts culminated in the 1983 book and traveling exhibition titled *From the Heart: Folk Art in Canada*, we had categorized everything under three themes: Reflection, Commitment and Fantasy. The patriotic materials fit nicely under Commitment, along with love and religion; three areas of powerful emotion. Donna and Nigel were valued friends and collaborators in those days when we struggled to define and collect Canadian folk art. One of the key objects in our exhibition was the Mountie quilt, pictured also in this book, which the museum acquired from the Hutchinses in 1977. That quilt gave focus to the patriotic section of the museum's collections and provided encouragement for us to pursue and collect many more examples of this important and fascinating genre.

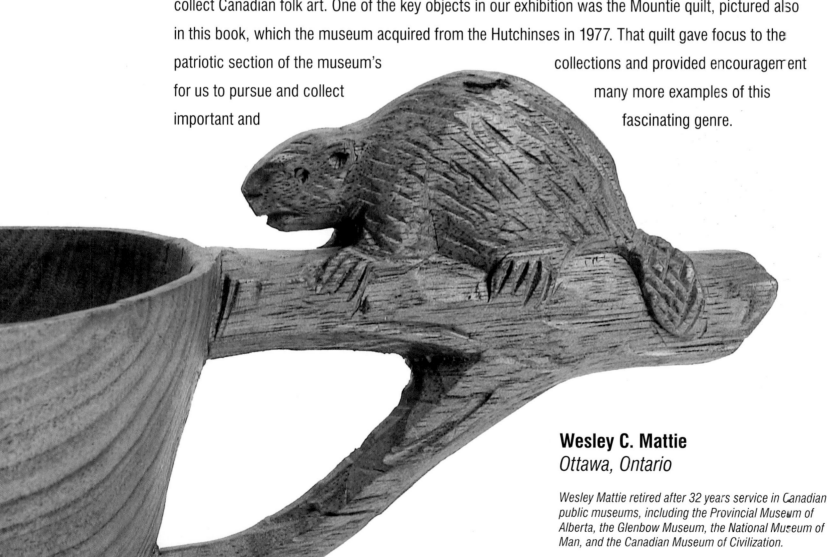

Wesley C. Mattie
Ottawa, Ontario

Wesley Mattie retired after 32 years service in Canadian public museums, including the Provincial Museum of Alberta, the Glenbow Museum, the National Museum of Man, and the Canadian Museum of Civilization.

INTRODUCTION

The unique and memorable Mountie
Quilt was created by Beth Craig from
Delta, Ontario, in 1975. Her purpose
was to honour the Royal Canadian
Mounted Police and to teach children
appreciation for the Mounties'
exceptional qualities: knowledge
and love of nature, bravery and
fairness. "The Mountie is the symbolic
embodiment of the highest Canadian
values." Collection of the Canadian
Museum of Civilization

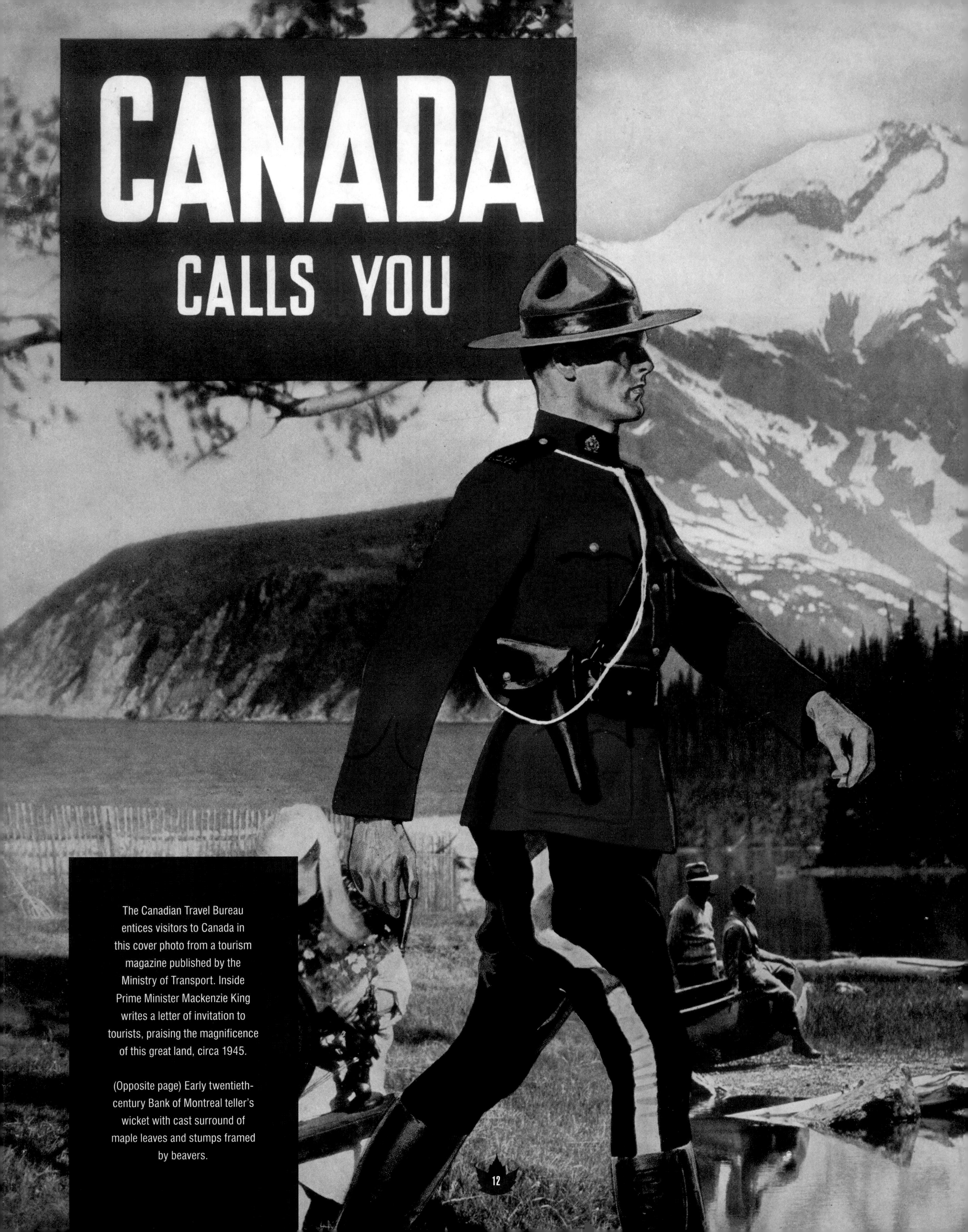

CANADA
CALLS YOU

The Canadian Travel Bureau entices visitors to Canada in this cover photo from a tourism magazine published by the Ministry of Transport. Inside Prime Minister Mackenzie King writes a letter of invitation to tourists, praising the magnificence of this great land, circa 1945.

(Opposite page) Early twentieth-century Bank of Montreal teller's wicket with cast surround of maple leaves and stumps framed by beavers.

INTRODUCTION

Patriotism is a powerful emotion that can be intoxicating when experienced with others. Most of us can recall vivid moments in our past when a particular belief took hold. These moments become imprinted on our psyche and are even more powerful when we realize that we share them with a multitude of other individuals. A patriotic group can effect compelling and awesome change. The history of a nation is reflected in the nature of its inhabitants' sense of identity. How do we tell our stories of exploration, wars, tragedies and great human discoveries? Our perspective on these events, as they unfold, is fuelled by the love of homeland and our fear of losing it.

With the exception of our aboriginal peoples, the population of Canada reflects the history of its immigration, whether we are first or tenth-generation Canadians. The seeds of my patriotism were planted when my grandparents, both maternal and paternal, left Poland at the turn of the twentieth century. They immigrated to Canada with the desire to begin a new life, just as their ancestors had fled from the guillotine during the French Revolution to a safer life in Poland. Nigel still remembers the "coal-black, rainy night" when he and his parents left on the ocean liner *Empress of Scotland* from the port of Southampton, England, to begin anew in Canada. His father, an officer in the British Royal Navy, had decided that their future would be better served if he transferred to the Canadian Navy, which, post WWII, was recruiting new officers. The stories that are told by our two families reflect the anxieties and aspirations of all immigrants to this vast country. One intrinsic goal that my grandparents and Nigel's parents shared was their common desire to assimilate into Canadian society as it evolved. They would not cling to their ethnicity by isolating themselves in miniature Polish or British communities. As Nigel's father explained: "This is our new home. We are no longer residents of England."

Nigel's excitement about coming to Canada was a sharp contrast to his mother's sense of loss at leaving her home. When he and his family landed in Quebec City, he eagerly expected to be greeted by Mounties. It wasn't until his first Dominion Day in Annapolis Royal that he finally saw these Canadian heroes in their red dress uniforms.

My first recollection of national pride took place in a grade-five geography class. We were studying Canada, what else? As I began to read about the beauty and vastness of this country, with its wealth of untapped natural resources, I felt intensely pleased and naïvely secure about our future. How could the rest of the world not see us as important and powerful, and did it matter anyway? To a ten year old it was *The Emperor's New Clothes* story, in reverse. Instead of wearing nothing, we were

dressed lavishly, but no one seemed to notice. I think we still have the opportunity to see ourselves from that perspective.

Like many other Canadians, we all have our memories of shared patriotic experiences. When 1967 arrived, my father and I, like many others, made a huge centennial symbol to hang at the front of our porch. That was a year when the country felt the most united "from sea to sea." There was no sense of disharmony as Quebec hosted our centennial party by inviting the world to a spectacular World's Fair. The colour and sophistication of Quebec culture ignited in me a desire to improve my French, even though I still cheered loudly when the Maple Leafs won the Stanley Cup that same year. The competition between Montreal and Toronto, particularly when played out on the hockey rink, has always been a safe and celebratory ritual of the English-French rivalry so infamous in Canada's history.

In my early years as a professional actress, I was engaged to bring theatre to rural schools, where I had many opportunities to experience this land. Our tours took us to rural communities in British Columbia and Ontario. The beauty of our country was enchanting, and the varieties of social experience were fascinating. As a "navy brat," Nigel grew up in cities and towns across Canada, from Victoria to Montreal, from Halifax to Ottawa, and his physical immersion in this land opened his eyes to its grandeur.

Nigel and I met while working in Canadian theatre. It wasn't long before his passion for collecting antiquities took hold of me as well. Our honeymoon was a journey to the Maritimes, and as we drove from Ottawa, through Quebec City, and all the way to Prince Edward Island, we searched for interesting collectables in the villages and along the country lanes that prosperity had left behind.

Jean Minhinnick, the late curator of Upper Canada Village, once referred to our generation as the "last to touch the hand that touched the hand." This comment could have included our grandparents, but it also applied to those of us fortunate enough to have travelled the rustic roads before modern society invaded the remote rural regions of this country.

Prior to the modern age, visual reference came from viewing the object, from memory, from nature or from following the traditions of European and American aesthetics. Early representations of the beaver, maple leaf and Mountie were, for the most part, traditional in form. Often they were incorporated into objects bearing images of our respective heritage, the fleur-de-lis or Union Jack. Early manufacturers of glass and china employed these symbols in their wares, and use of these elements in print was widespread.

Two historic events changed Canadians' sense of their country dramatically in the twentieth

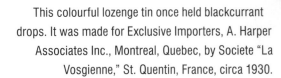

This colourful lozenge tin once held blackcurrant drops. It was made for Exclusive Importers, A. Harper Associates Inc., Montreal, Quebec, by Societe "La Vosgienne," St. Quentin, France, circa 1930.

century. Canada had long been considered a colony of England, therefore our flag, as with those of other Commonwealth nations, included the Union Jack as a key design element. The Second World War exposed our troops to the world, and upon their return, many who had fought so valiantly under the Red Ensign yearned for a flag that was uniquely Canadian. In 1965, after riotous debate, Canadians finally adopted a flag bearing the red maple leaf. In 1967, when Montreal hosted the World's Fair, Expo ´67, works by Canadian designers, craftsmen and artists were prominently displayed and were no longer viewed as an extension of European aesthetic models. Instead, a uniquely Canadian movement in form and style was emerging, one which had begun with the Group of Seven 40 years earlier.

This blossoming of form moved our symbols from their traditional roots into a new era. Gordon Lightfoot, Ian and Sylvia, Felix Leclerc and Gilles Vigneault painted musical pictures of our great land, the latter two awakening the spirit of a Quebec society justly seeking its place as an equal partner at the Canadian table. Could the high of Expo ´67 not be maintained in such a multicultural nation?

It was in the 1980s that Nigel and I became concerned about the future of our country's survival. At that time it was certainly not "cool" to be Canadian. The fragility of our nation was exacerbated by the most radical of separatists in Quebec, the increase in the Americanization of Anglo-Canadian culture, fears over the effects of free trade, and a general apathy among Canadians. It seemed at times that those who cared about a united country were becoming a dwindling minority.

In this climate of indifference and fragmentation, I suggested to Nigel that we redirect our collecting by changing our focus from the exceptional to Canadian symbols in all forms, kitsch, high art, folk art and commercial branding. We both hoped that, in the future, our country's identity might attain a more noble status, and, if not, these pieces would at least survive as remnants of a splintered Canadian dream.

The pivotal catalyst for this endeavour was our discovery of the Mountie Quilt at a Christmas Craft Fair in Ottawa. The artist, Beth Craig from Delta, Ontario, had created a large quilt bordered by red maple leaves. The body consisted of hand-painted scenes of the red-coated Mounties doing good deeds. The quilt was anything but traditional in form or technical execution, but it was brilliant! Years later, we were proud to see this piece featured as a major inclusion in the Museum of Civilization's national exhibit "From the Heart."

Our symbols exist for all Canadians. They do not represent a particular ethnic background or culture or creed. They are available to everyone who decides to live in this country and claim citizenship. They are iconic expressions of this country's identity, an identity that often seems elusive.

Titled "King of the West," this guitar was manufactured for distribution through a mail-order catalogue in the 1950s, when Mounties and cowboys were popular heroic figures.

Nigel is a ferocious picker. From his early work as a decorator in Montreal and his later studies at the National Theatre School, he developed a keen interest in the tangible objects that reflect our culture. It was always the graphic image that drove his collecting instincts. Sugar moulds with maple leaves, bells with beavers, beaver sealers — these items, while not related, possess a visual continuity. Without his determination and energy, this project would never have evolved. He was able to sniff out collectable gems in the most unlikely places.

It soon became evident to us that the three symbols of the maple leaf, the beaver and the Mountie held the greatest historical significance for most Canadians. They are the recurring elements most often used by corporations and souvenir manufacturers to signify our Canadian identity. If branding with an icon attributes certain qualities to a company, then those companies that adopt one or all three symbols in their advertising thereby promise a Canadian ideal to their consumers.

In the past ten years, a new generation of Canadians has emerged. The Molson "I AM CANADIAN" ad campaign expressed a patriotism that is less defensive and more exclamatory. We see this among our sons' peers. They do not see themselves as the wallflowers at a school prom, watching their U.S. cousins steal the limelight. They are proudly Canadian. The last few summers I have taken the time to create in our front yard a Canadian flag made from red and white impatiens. The effort is well worth it when I hear neighbours tell me that it brings smiles to their faces, or when children ride by on their bikes and slow down to look at the "flag of flowers."

We hope that this book will cause you to slow down and smile, too.

Perched on a ship vent, this beaver appears more like his unpopular cousin, the rat. In the early 1900s the Canadian Merchant Marine displayed a beaver on their House Flag and became known as the Rat Line.

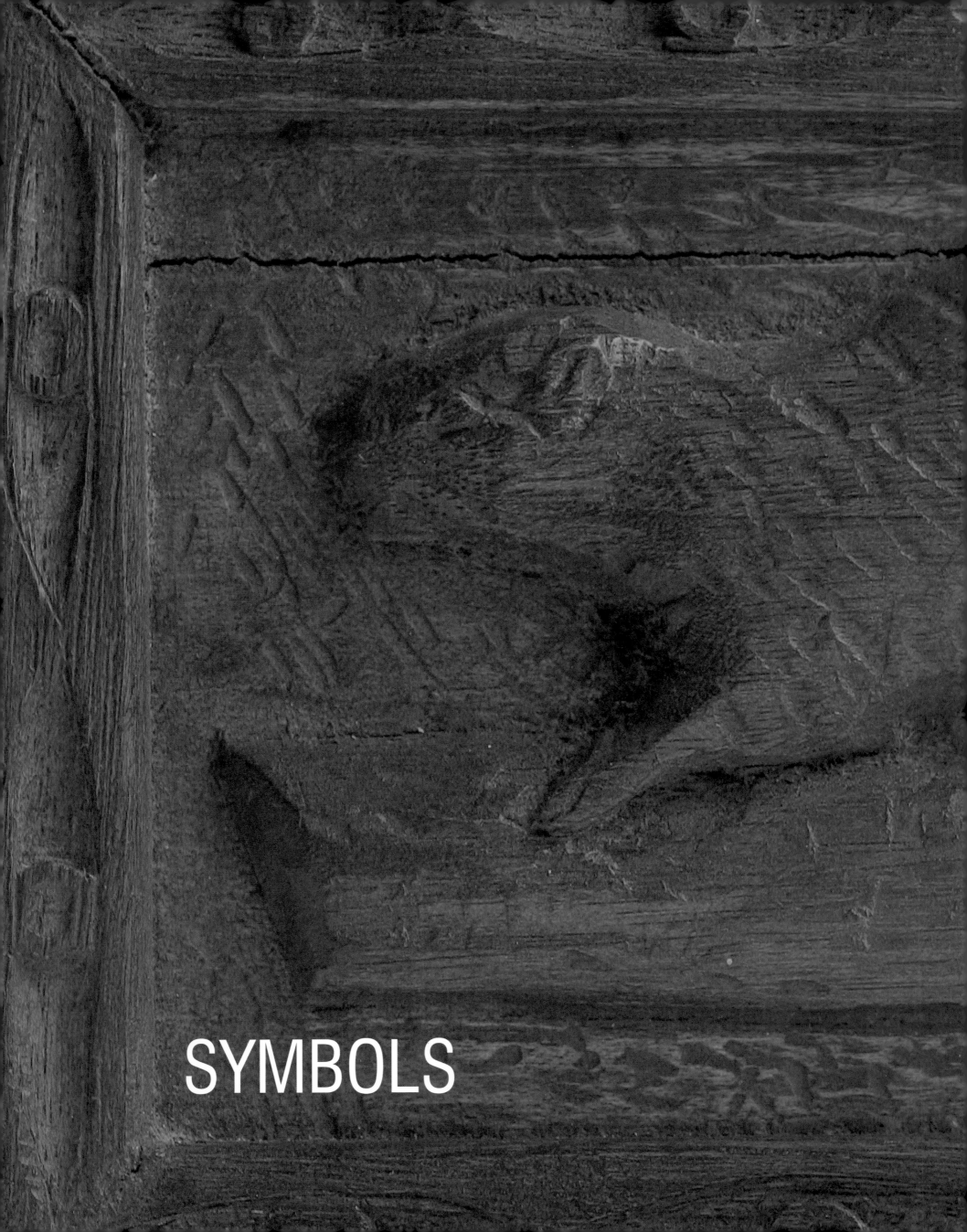

SYMBOLS

This hand-carved
late-nineteenth-century
wooden beaver panel
was the lid for a
corncob-holder box.

THE MAPLE LEAF

For as long as we can determine, humans have used symbols as a form of individual and group expression. Symbols give meaning and understanding to our lives. They often speak a universal language that, according to Carl Jung, is embedded in the "collective unconscious." It has been discovered that many ancient civilizations — living in isolated communities, oceans and continents apart — in fact used almost identical symbols in their cave drawings.

The implementation of symbols is a timeless phenomenon. Whenever humans gather together for a common goal, they invariably choose an icon to represent their purpose. Organizations, whether casual or structured, will select identical colours, clothing and/or emblems to identify themselves as members. The unifying bond may be further expressed in song or a special gesture. Symbols play a significant role in establishing group identity and often evoke senses of pride and belonging in the individuals who are members. It is no wonder that when a country comes into being, part of the identity process becomes the choosing of an anthem and a national flag, even a symbolic animal or flower.

A nation's choice of symbols often becomes a paradigm for how its citizens see themselves. The mighty eagle expresses the United States' confidence and sense of power; the dragon is a fierce and ancient animal that suggests China's strength and its ancient mystery; England's lion denotes the regal dominance of an empire that once ruled the seas.

Throughout our history, Canadians have chosen common symbols linked to the history of this great land. It would be argued by some that Canada has indeed a multiplicity of identifying emblems. In the July 2, 2005, issue of the *Toronto Star,* Conrad Biernacki wrote, "…a list of iconic symbols of Canada begins with the four Ms: mountains, moose, Mounties and the maple leaf. These are followed by the beaver, loon, Canada goose and Inukshuk."

While all of these may imply a Canadian uniqueness, we have elected to focus on the three that are the most recognizable to the rest of the world as the symbols of this country: the maple leaf, the beaver and the Mountie.

The maple leaf flies proudly from our flag and is synonymous with "made in Canada"; the beaver has been emblazoned on countless items, from currency to clothing, since fur-trading days; and the Mounties are legendary — as much for their colourful dress uniforms as for their mythical heroism. What do these symbols represent to us? What do they reveal in terms of our national character? We think that it is useful to look at the symbols' historical relevance, because they tell the story of our nation and in the process they reveal our character.

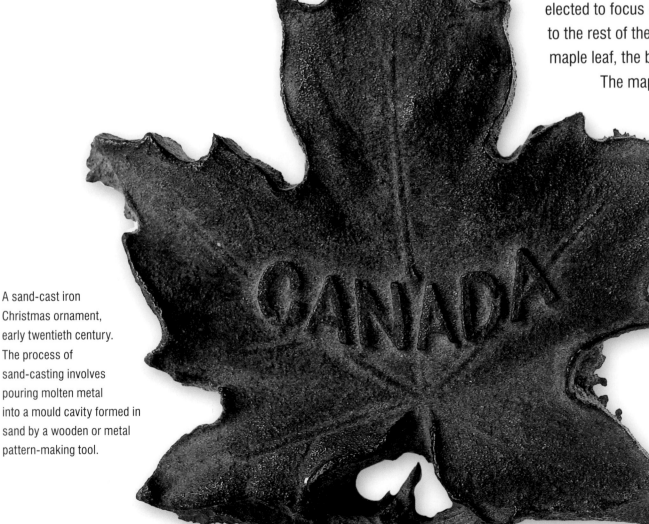

A sand-cast iron Christmas ornament, early twentieth century. The process of sand-casting involves pouring molten metal into a mould cavity formed in sand by a wooden or metal pattern-making tool.

THE MAPLE LEAF

Long before the arrival of European explorers and settlers, aboriginal peoples inhabited this vast land we now call Canada. When Jacques Cartier came here in 1535, he referred to the land east of the St. Lawrence by its Native name, Kanata, meaning "village." The Natives' spiritual belief in an integrated relationship between humankind and the Earth caused most indigenous people to be sensitive and appreciative of the abundance of natural resources. Maple trees were plentiful in the massive eastern forests and were considered a precious resource. The Natives had countless uses for these trees, and they shared their knowledge with the early colonialists. Not only did the wood offer sturdy shelter, the sap that ran from the sugar maple in the spring offered nourishment as a food source. European settlers soon learned how to create maple syrup and maple-sugar candy, a knowledge that would eventually lead to the development of a substantial industry.

Despite its many uses, the maple has always been admired for its beauty. The maple tree in its autumn splendour is nearly as inspiring for those on a scenic drive through the countryside as it is for the poets, artists and photographers who perennially try to capture the majesty of colour in the autumn landscape.

Historians believe that the maple leaf was used symbolically to represent this country as early as the beginning of the eighteenth century. The St-Jean-Baptiste Society adopted the symbol of the maple leaf in 1834. Le Canadien, a Lower Canada newspaper, decided in 1836 that the maple leaf was a suitable emblem for Canada. The Toronto literary annual *The Maple Leaf* called it the chosen emblem of Canada in 1848. The 100th Regiment of Royal Canadians used the maple leaf as their badge in 1860, and in that same year the citizens of Upper Canada were asked to wear maple leaves as emblems of Canada to welcome the Prince of Wales to this country. It is no wonder then that Alexander Muir's song "The Maple Leaf Forever" became our first national anthem, in celebration of our Confederation in 1867. (The fact that his song was never popular in Quebec may have something to do with the lyrics: "God save our Queen and heaven bless the Maple Leaf Forever.")

In 1868 both Ontario and Quebec included a maple leaf in their coats of arms. When Canada finally issued its own coins in 1876, the maple leaf appeared on all denominations and remained so until 1901. Today's penny still shows the double maple leaf. In the First World War the maple leaf was included in the badge of the Canadian Expeditionary Forces, and during the Second World War it was used by the forces on badges and equipment.

In 1921 the maple leaf was firmly ensconced as a Canadian symbol when it was assigned to Canada in the official coat of arms proclaimed by King George V. At this time the use of red and white as Canada's official colours was also made official. The French and English had used these colours dating back to the Crusades in the eleventh century. For a time, France had displayed a red cross on its banners, while England had displayed a white cross. In 1965, at the urging of then Prime Minister Lester B. Pearson, the maple leaf and the national colours came together as the official flag of Canada: "...this flag...will stand for one Canada; united strong and independent and equal to her tasks."

One of a pair of unsigned bronze bookends found in upper New York State, dating from the early twentieth century.

This T. Eaton Company souvenir program features on its cover Alexander Muir, author of the song "The Maple Leaf Forever." Timothy Eaton, an Irish immigrant, founded his very popular department store in 1869 when he opened a small dry-goods store in Toronto. By the early twentieth century, the Eaton empire was a thriving mail-order business with retail stores across Canada. But by the end of the twentieth century, the company's fortunes had diminished greatly, and one of Eaton's old rivals, Sears Canada, purchased all of its outstanding shares in 1999.

One of a pair of synthetic wood bookends, circa 1920.

THE BEAVER

The First People have always had a strong relationship with the beaver. Many of the Six Nations tribes have beaver clans, and the beaver is even a sign in the Native zodiac. Beaver clan people are considered very industrious and said to love to help others. For those born under the beaver sign (April 4-May 20), "possession means security" and their life purpose is "recognition and possession of lasting values." But beavers need to develop "flexibility, sympathy and initiative." Perhaps Canadians are more like beavers than we have previously acknowledged.

The first Europeans came to this land seeking gold and the riches of the Orient. Instead what they discovered was a vast, unexplored continent. Before the Native tribes began trading beaver pelts for the white man's goods, the trapping of beavers was done for the purpose of survival. The beaver was sought after for its pelts, which provided great comfort from the damp cold of winter, and its meat, which had nutritional and medicinal properties. In the late 1600s European fashion declared fur hats a necessity, and as this fashion grew, the demand for beaver pelts grew with it.

The French saw the fur industry as an opportunity to create wealth and to establish a new empire in North America. The English, meanwhile, saw Canada as part of the British Empire. Demand for beaver pelts fuelled the need for further exploration of this country. The English formed the Hudson's Bay Company in 1671 to continue exploration in search of ever more beaver pelts. The French Montreal-based Northwest Company had a similar mandate. (The Northwest Company and the Hudson's Bay Company would amalgamate in 1821.) As early as 1635 the Jesuits had already observed the beaver's potential extinction due to over-trapping. Had it not been for the greed of the traders, who continued to inflate the price of pelts, and the fact that European fashion trends eventually embraced silk hats, we may not have the beaver (*castor Canadensis*) with us today.

Even before the use of the maple leaf, as early as the 1600s, the beaver was used by both French and English as an emblem of Canada. The Hudson's Bay Company included four beavers in their 1678 coat of arms. The victory medal of France, Kebeca Liberata, of 1690, featured a beaver on its reverse side. Though the fur trade declined, the beaver continued to be used as a symbol, often in conjunction with the maple leaf. In 1851 the beaver was given the privilege of being featured on the first Canadian postage stamp, and it can still be found on our nickel. The idea that beavers are industrious and conscientious has encouraged their inclusion in the logos of many organizations and corporations. However, it wasn't until March 24, 1975, that the beaver finally attained official status as "a symbol of the sovereignty of Canada."

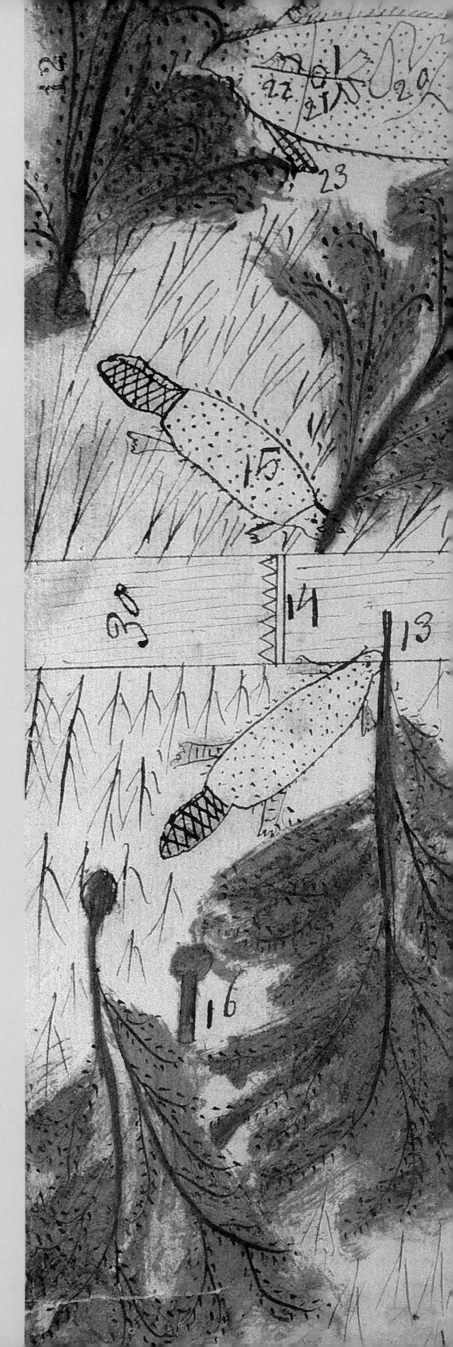

A naïve painting of a fur trapper reproduced for the June 1945 cover of the Hudson's Bay Company magazine, *The Beaver*. The original 1743 watercolour-and-ink work, entitled *Hunting Beaver*, was done by then HBC governor James Isham.

How the Beaver Got His Tail
An Ojibwa Legend

Once upon a time there was a beaver that loved to brag about his tail.

One day while taking a walk, the beaver stopped to talk to a bird. The beaver said to the bird, "Don't you love my fluffy tail?"

"Why, yes I do little beaver," replied the bird.

"Don't you wish your feathers were as fluffy as my tail? Don't you wish your feathers were as strong as my tail? Don't you wish your feathers were just as beautiful as my tail?" the beaver asked.

"Why do you think so much of your tail, little beaver?" asked the bird. This insulted the beaver and he walked away.

After walking for a while, he stopped for a drink by the river and saw a muskrat. He walked to the muskrat and said, "Hello little muskrat. What do you think about my tail?"

"Well, it is very beautiful and big and fluffy," answered the muskrat. "Is it also a strong tail?"

"Why, yes it is," the beaver answered. "Do you wish you had a tail like mine?"

"I didn't say I wanted a tail like yours. I just asked if it was strong," the muskrat replied with a disgusted voice.

The beaver quickly turned and began walking back to the dam. He was very angry because he felt that the animals were being rude to him. He was very upset and decided to take out his frustration by cutting down trees. After cutting down a couple of trees, he came to a very large one. He knew that it would be a great challenge for him. So he went to it. But as he was cutting, he kept thinking about his tail and didn't notice that he was cutting at a bad angle. Before he knew what was happening, the tree began to fall toward him. He jumped to get out of the way, but he didn't jump fast enough, and the huge tree fell on his beautiful tail! He tugged and pulled and finally dug away the earth to free himself. When he finally pulled his tail from under the tree, he was horrified to see that it was flat. The beaver was very sad and started to cry. As he was crying he heard a voice. It was the Creator.

"Why are you crying?" asked the Creator.

"A tree has crushed my beautiful tail," the beaver cried. "Now no one will like me."

The Creator told him that a beaver is not liked for his tail but for his kindness and wisdom. He also told him how to use his flat tail. "Now your tail will help you swim rapidly," the Creator said. "And when you want to signal a friend, all you have to do is slap your tail on the water."

Hearing this made the beaver happy again. When the animals saw his flattened tail they were shocked! But the beaver said, "It's better this way."

From that day on the beaver never bragged about his tail, and all the animals liked him.

That's how the beaver got his tail.

A stuffed beaver in a natural maquette, private collection, circa 1950.

PRO PELLE CUTEM

HBC 1670

275th Anniversary HBC

The Beaver

A MAGAZINE OF THE NORTH

PUBLISHED QUARTERLY BY Hudson's Bay Company. OUTFIT 276 JUNE 1945
INCORPORATED 2ⁿᵈ MAY 1670

Vol. I MARCH, 1921 No. 6

The Beaver
A Journal of Progress

H.B.C.

Laden with skins from the north,
Beaver and bear and raccoon,
Marten and mink from the polar belts,
Otter and ermine and sable pelts—
The spoils of the hunter's moon.
—Pauline Johnson.

Devoted to The Interests of Those Who Serve The Hudson's Bay Company

(Opposite page) *The Beaver* magazine was established in 1920 to celebrate the 250th anniversary of the Hudson's Bay Company. This anniversary issue features the original HBC coat of arms on the cover. The motto *pro pelle cutem* translates as "a skin for a skin," suggesting the dangers facing the fur trader.

(Above) A fur trapper returning home for the night. This was the March 1921 cover of *The Beaver*. The author of the poem is Pauline Johnson, one of Canada's most famous historical personalities. The daughter of an English mother and a Mohawk father, Johnson was the first Native poet to have her work published in Canada.

THE MOUNTIE

Like any national police force, the Royal Canadian Mounted Police has its critics as well as its admirers. It is interesting that Americans, particularly those in the Hollywood film industry, have always shown a fondness for the "red coats," portraying them as a gentler, kinder cousin to the all-American hero. It is safe to say that the Mounties are probably the least maligned police force in the world. Whether accurate or not, the image of a Mountie conjures up qualities such as courage, civility, caring and persistence.

The force began its life as the Northwest Mounted Police, established in 1873 by Sir John A. Macdonald to bring order to the land that ran from the western border of Manitoba to the Rockies and north. The combination of unscrupulous fur-traders, Aboriginal tribes threatened by loss of territory, and terrified land-grant settlers led to a general sense of lawlessness. The Canadian government needed a police force in order to complete the Canadian Pacific Railway that would link the country together. The Mounties were invaluable, not just for keeping the peace. In those early years they also delivered mail, kept records of births, deaths and even weather. When gold was discovered in the Yukon, the force had to recruit new members to handle the vast territories and throngs of goldseekers.

By 1904 King Edward VII granted the use of the term "Royal" in their title, and they became the Royal North West Mounted Police. It wasn't until 1920, when they absorbed the Dominion Police, that they became the Royal Canadian Mounted Police. Today, Ontario and Quebec are the only provinces that do not use the RCMP as their provincial police force. In his book The Mountie from Dime Novel to Disney, author Michael Dawson suggests that the mythical image of the Mountie is in fact the English-Canadian perspective. He suggests that the Aboriginal or the French-Canadian viewpoints would tell a very different story. Whatever the truth, through the spinning of stories and legend, the Mountie has evolved into a Canadian hero known the world over, much as the cowboy became a folk hero of the American West.

Items featuring the red-coated Mountie have long been favourite souvenirs of this country. The Mounted Police Foundation was established in 1995 to address the issue of unlicensed products and their potential harm to the Mountie image. That same year the Disney Corporation was granted a five-year contract to handle the marketing and licensing of RCMP products, on behalf of the new foundation, which lacked expertise in corporate imaging. The Mounted Police Foundation now operates this program itself, and since 2002 has granted over a million dollars from royalties on products to community programs and projects focused on safety for all Canadians.

Canada's symbols have evolved through the telling of the Canadian story. If they are a paradigm for the Canadian identity, then they tell the story of a people often ridiculed; a people who are stubborn and industrious, versatile, strong and beautiful, and sometimes even a bit pompous about their virtuosity. Yet any arrogance that we might feel about our country is usually tempered with humour and tolerance. When we can begin to see ourselves as a nation unto itself, and not as one in competition with the United States or any other super power, then perhaps we will be at peace with our own identity. Perhaps then we will be able to embrace our symbols and the stories that they represent. They can then truly be the iconic representations of our Canadian identity.

(Right) Leather badge
from child's costume,
circa 1950.

(Bottom) The figures in
this chorus of Canada's
finest were manufactured
by Regal, Canada,
circa 1950.

Manufacturing sources for Canada's souvenirs are as multicultural as the nation's population. Until the RCMP established their licensing program in 1995, anyone could brand the image of a Mountie to their product. Many of these figures were created offshore. At front, from left to right: a metal Mountie on horseback, with "Main le Droit" inscribed on the base; "I am a Rogark Doll," made in North Wales; Mountie on horseback, made in England; porcelain Mountie, made in Japan; Aboriginal Mountie on wooden base with felt uniform; Kewpie doll Mountie; Wobble-Head Mountie; wooden Mountie bank (press the chimney and the coin slot is revealed); carved wooden folk-art Mountie; standing Mountie (behind Dudley), made in Hong Kong; (bottom) "Dudley Do-Right" rubber doll, made in Hong Kong by Jesco; standing doll with material uniform, made by the Alexander Doll Company, New York. The other figures were manufactured by Regal, Canada.

CANADA

COMMERCE

An early nineteenth-century wooden maple-sugar mould from Quebec. The spring ritual of "sugaring off" led to a diverse range of maple products, including maple sugar, maple syrup and maple butter. Early settlers often used Canadian symbols such as the beaver and the maple leaf in their product packaging.

The popularity of beaver hats in Europe drove the Canadian trapping industry and ultimately led to settlement across Canada. (Bottom left) A nineteenth-century Welsh hat with silk bow.

(Top right) A late-nineteenth-century English top hat. Both hats are from the collection of the Canadian Museum of Civilization.

(Top left) A hand-forged spearhead from the Northwest Fur Trading Company of 1782. In 1779 the Métis Nation, in partnership with trading firms in Montreal, established their own company. The Native people of the northern forests found it more convenient to trade with this company than to make the journey up to Hudson Bay. The Northwest Company refused to recognize the Hudson's Bay Company's monopoly, and so the two continued to forge their respective ways through the river systems of Canada, establishing rival forts along the way, and reaching the Rocky Mountains by the 1800s. Despite the fact that by 1795 the HBC was responsible for just one-fifth of the total fur harvest, they still held control of the main port on Hudson Bay. After a bitter and often violent rivalry, the two companies merged on March 26, 1821.

(Bottom right) A wooden beaver maple-sugar mould from Quebec, mid-nineteenth century.

This plaque commemorates the 1947 convention of the Cosmopolitan International Club in Banff, Alberta. This service club, established in 1927, has a network of 78 member clubs located in Canada, the USA and Mexico. The Calgary chapter was created in 1930. Their mission is to contribute to community well-being through charitable donations and volunteer service, with special emphasis on supporting efforts to prevent and find a cure for diabetes. On the back of this souvenir is written: "This plaque is a Canadian product — the woods of our North country supply the pulp; our prairies the chemicals; our mines the machinery and equipment of production; and the mighty Niagara the power…."

(Right) "Visit Us in Hamilton," a souvenir item commemorating George V, King of England from 1910 to 1936.

(Below) When the Dominion of Canada was formed in 1867, the Canadian government had to assume responsibility for its currency and banking system. The first coinage was issued in denominations of 1, 5, 10, 25 and 50 cents. This large one-cent piece from 1906 features a garland of maple leaves, while this 1922 five-cent piece shows a pair of maple leaves. The beaver has appeared on Canadian five-cent coins (nickel) since 1937.

(Bottom) This cheque was issued in the 1930s by the the Imperial Bank of Canada which had been established in Toronto in 1875. In 1961, the largest merger of two chartered banks in Canadian history occurred when this bank merged with the Canadian Bank of Commerce to become the Canadian Imperial Bank of Commerce.

A Beaver Brand butter box from the early twentieth century. The Beaver Brand trademark
was registered in 1927 by Canada Packers Inc., Toronto. In the late nineteenth century,
Ontario was the main agricultural producer in Canada. The Crow's Nest Pass Agreement
of 1897 led to western domination of the agricultural industry. This agreement gave
competitive advantage to the eastbound movement of Canadian grain.

UNITED WE STAND. DIVIDED WE FALL.
SCOTT'S EMULSION
STRENGTHENS ALL.

BACK OF CALENDAR · CHROMOLITHOGRAPH PROOF · CANADA EPHEMERA COLLECTION

(Top) This stunning chromo-lithograph proof was used by the Ephemera Society of Canada as the back page for a calendar. The original was created in 1899 for Scott's Emulsion.

(Right) A mid-twentieth-century cast-metal paperweight souvenir from the Callander Company, a maker of power tools in Guelph, Ontario.

Maple Leaf Mills has been called "the company that grew with Canada" and can trace its history back to one of the first flour mills in Ontario, Grantham Mills, which was built in St. Catharines, Ontario, in 1836. In 1904 Maple Leaf Flour Mills Company Limited was formed, and in 1907 they acquired Hedley Shaw Milling Company Limited (including Grantham Mills). Three years later, the Maple Leaf Milling Company Limited was formed as a merger of mills in Kenora, Brandon, St. Catharines and Thorold, as well as 40 grain elevators in the western provinces. The Maple Leaf Mills Limited was officially formed in 1961 from an amalgamation of Maple Leaf Milling Company Limited of Toronto, Elevators Limited and Purity Flour Mills Ltd. The Maple Leaf Foods Inc. of today was formed through the merger of Maple Leaf Mills Limited and Canada Packers Inc. in 1991.

Maple Leaf Milling designed a colourful logo to make its diverse line of agricultural products easily identifiable. Here we see the sack from their Monarch Pig Starter. The old Maple Leaf Milling Company building in Toronto was demolished in 1983.

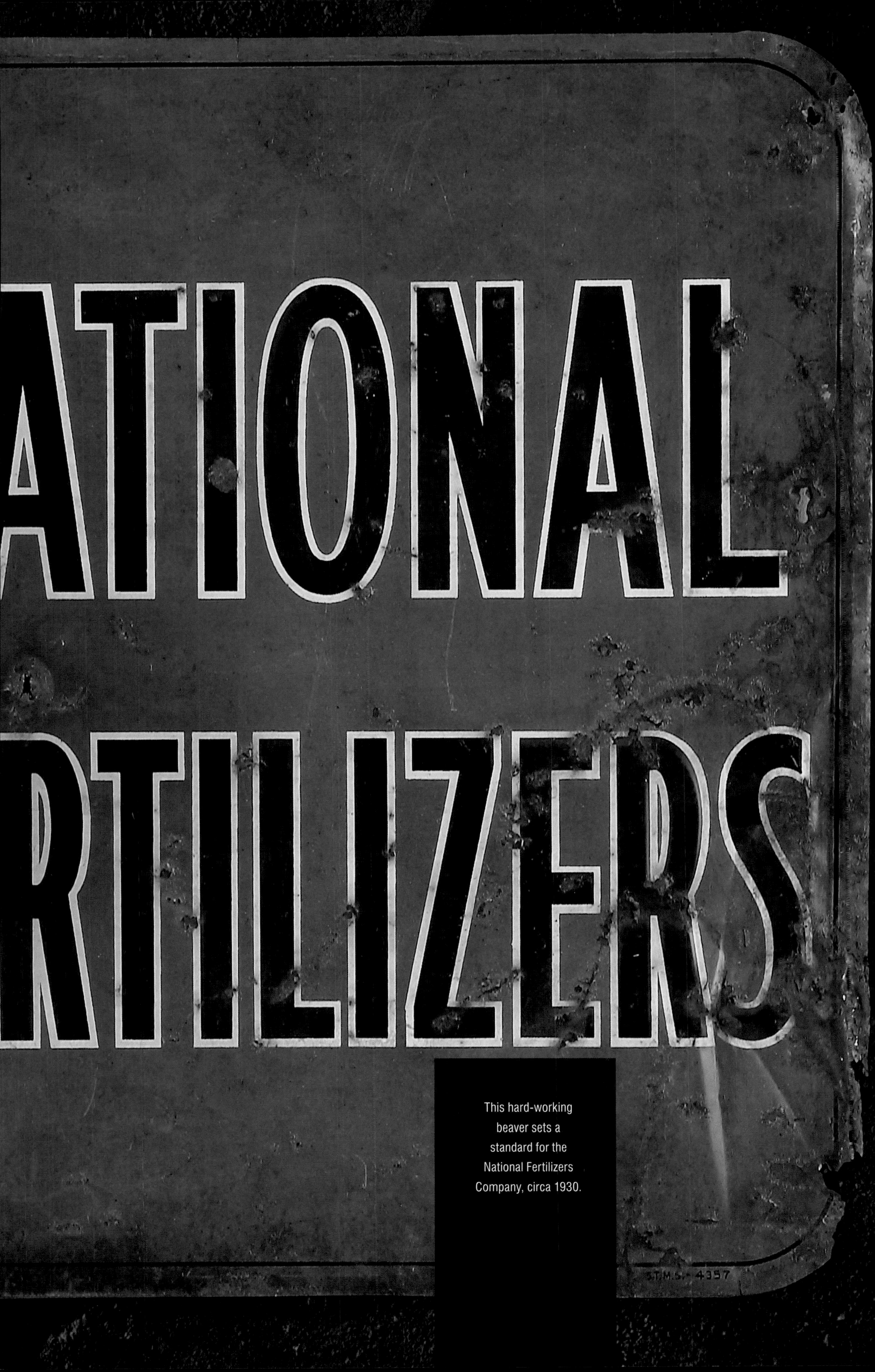

ATIONAL

RTILIZERS

This hard-working
beaver sets a
standard for the
National Fertilizers
Company, circa 1930.

S.T.M.S.- 4357

An early twentieth-century peanut-butter container from W. Clark Ltd.
of Montreal. This company, which manufactured prepared foods, was
established by Henry Clark in 1878 on Amherst Street in Montreal.

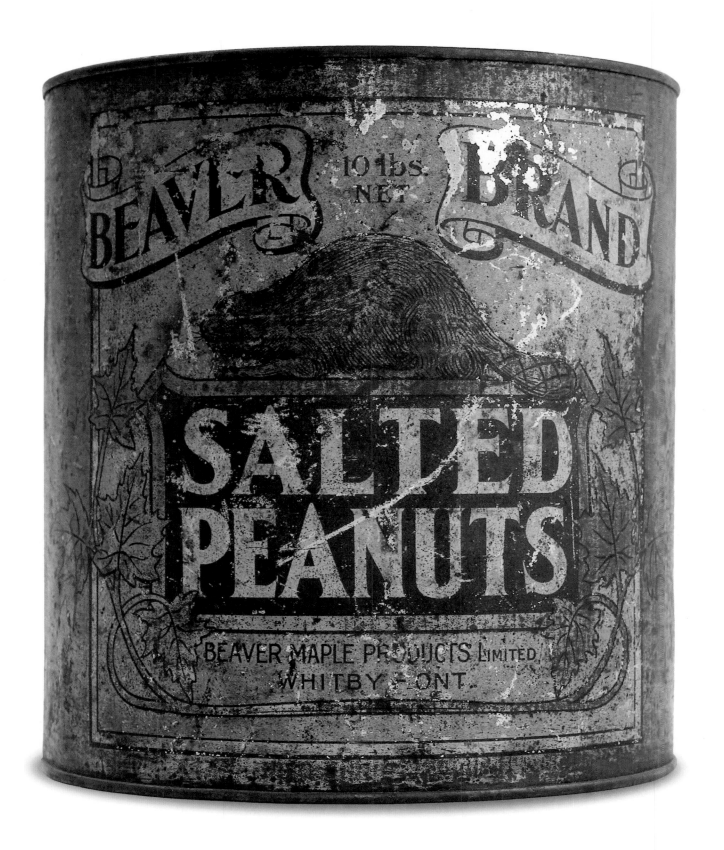

A Beaver Brand salted peanuts tin from Beaver
Maple Products, Whitby, Ontario, early twentieth
century.

(Top) Robertson Bros. Ltd., Toronto, produced these amusing and colourful tins to house their confectionery products. Five brothers founded this company in 1868. They started off making baked goods, as well as confections, but eventually specialized in "sweeties because they were more fun to eat." In 1873 they moved their company to the corner of Jarvis and Queen Streets, Toronto, where they remained for over 75 years. In 1973 the building became part of the Queen Street Mental Health Complex.

(Bottom) Beaver Brand maple butter was produced by Beaver Maple Products Ltd. in Whitby, Ontario.

An early twentieth-century confectionery tin featuring beavers, maple leaves and a garland of the nine provinces' shields (prior to the addition of Newfoundland as Canada's tenth province in 1949). Walter's Imperial toffee selection was manufactured by Walter's "Palm" Toffee Ltd., London, England, as a "Souvenir of Canada."

A collection of twentieth-century containers featuring beavers and maple leaves. The practice of canning edible items began in Europe in the early nineteenth century. In Canada, the joining of six smaller operations led to the formation of Canadian Canners Ltd. in 1903. Manufacturers hoped to entice buyers to their products by creating visually appealing labels. Skilled, but uncredited, artists were employed to accomplish this task. These early decorative manufacturing containers are very difficult to find in good condition and have thus become highly prized collectables. The circa-1900 Choice Teas tin is actually hand-stenciled and still in excellent condition.

Drewry's Ginger Ale was formed in 1877 and had its origins in Drewry's Lake of the Woods Brewery in Winnipeg, Manitoba. This 1920 sign features the Mountie, who continued to be used in their advertising. In the 1960s Drewry's bottled a root beer called "Drewry's Mountie," a popular item that was discontinued when the RCMP expressed their displeasure. The company was eventually bought by Pittsburgh Brewing Company, and the production of Drewry beverages came to an end.

(Below) John J. McLaughlin was manufacturing carbonated beverages, in Toronto, as early as 1890. In 1904 this company created a new ginger ale formula, for market, under the name "Canada Dry". It was so popular that they opened a firm in Edmonton Alberta. The business was incorporated by J.J. McLaughlin Ltd. in 1912 and eventually acquired by Canada Dry Ginger Ale Inc., New York in 1922. This company was eventually acquired by Cadbury Schweppes group of companies.

(Opposite page) Millennium-edition six-pack featuring the original packaging.

Marvin & Judy Chambers
PURE MAPLE PRODUCTS
R.R. 3, Waterford, Ontario
DE 1Y0 – (519) 443-8561

If you drive through the wooded countryside in the springtime, you may notice telltale lines or buckets suspended from the trunks of sugar maple trees. Farmers are tapping the trees for sap, which will be converted into numerous treats for consumers. Maple syrup production is still, in many cases, a family affair and has been throughout the years.

(Top) Maple leaf-shaped bottle, circa 2006.

(Bottom right) Old Colony Maple Syrup bottle, circa 1920.

(Bottom left) Novelty CN Tower maple syrup bottle, circa 2005.

(Left) Pop culture continues to identify itself with Canadian pride by using the maple leaf as a branding device. Pringles celebrates Canada in a July 1 promotional contest.

Two great ones! This Pepsi can features Wayne Gretzky at the 1978 World Junior Championships. In this particular tournament Wayne won the MVP and achieved 17 points in 6 games. Courtesy of Wayne Gretzky and the Wayne Gretzky Foundation

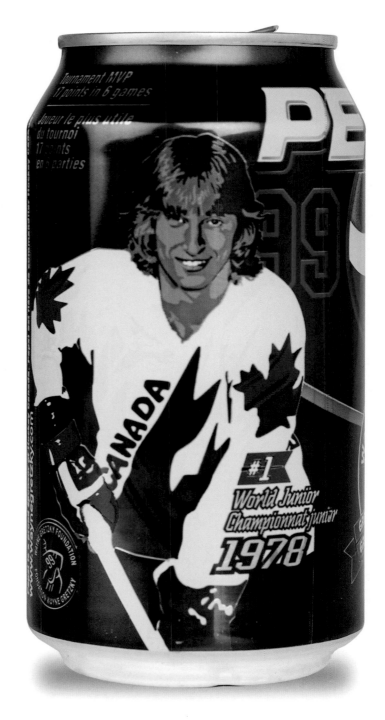

POLITICS

Maple leaf detailing from
the "Nine Province Flag"
of 1907.

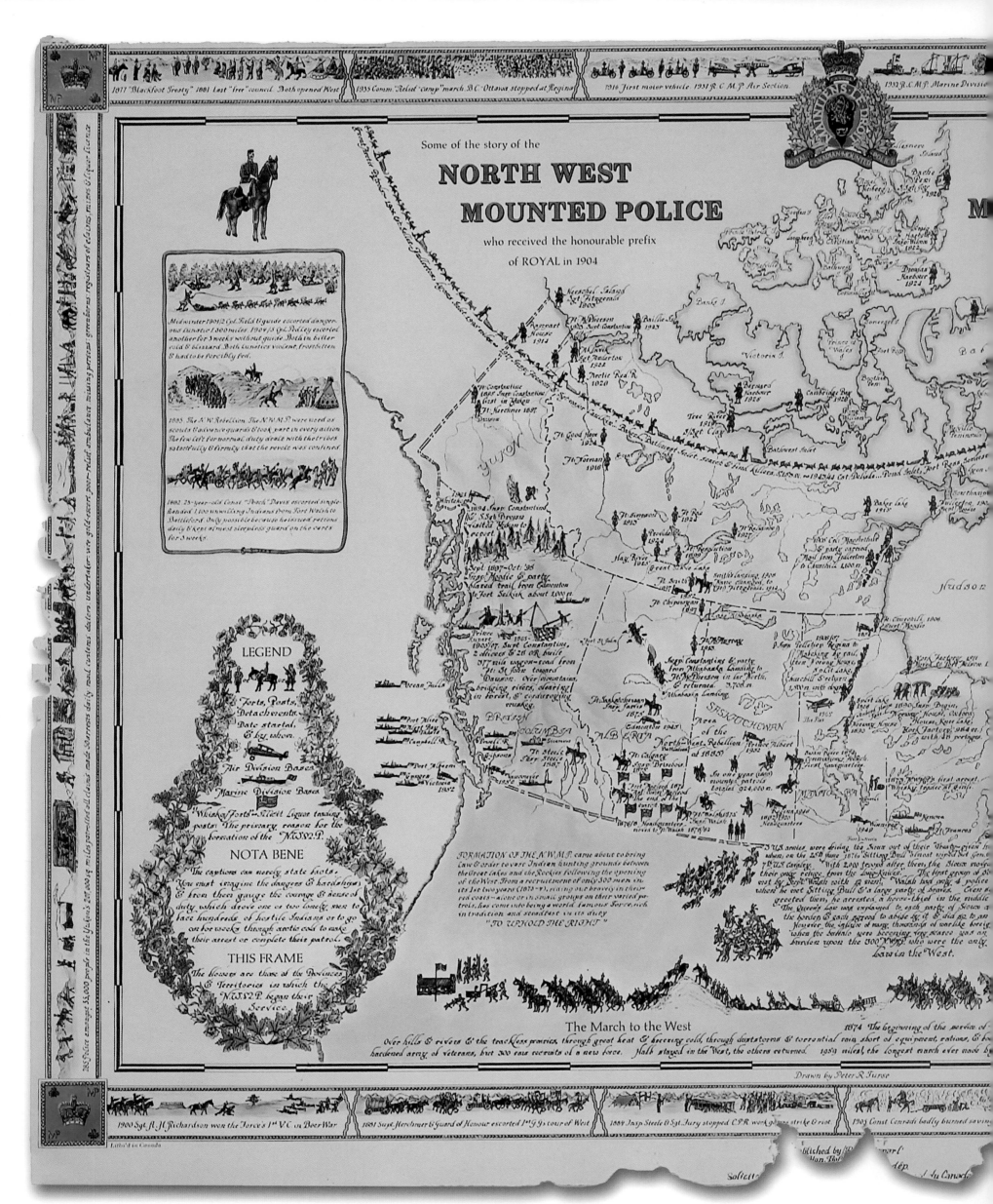

Some of the story of the

NORTH WEST
MOUNTED POLICE

who received the honourable prefix
of ROYAL in 1904

The March to the West

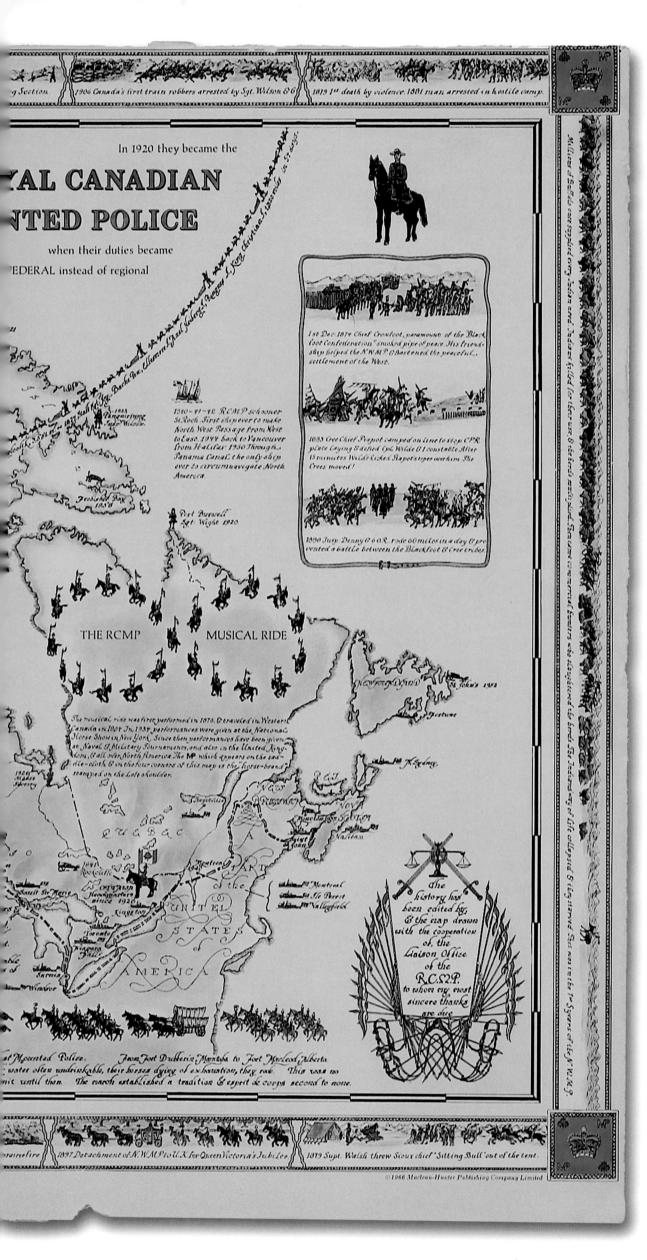

This collectable map showing the history of the RCMP was drawn by Peter R. Furse and produced by the Maclean Hunter Publications Company in 1966. Mr. Furse, a mapmaker from New Brunswick, was born in England and joined the Royal Navy at the age of 12. After many years at sea, he settled temporarily in South Africa until political unrest in that country drove him to the tranquility of the Canadian Maritimes. His talents as a mapmaker led to national recognition.

1873–1973
100 YEARS
OF SERVICE

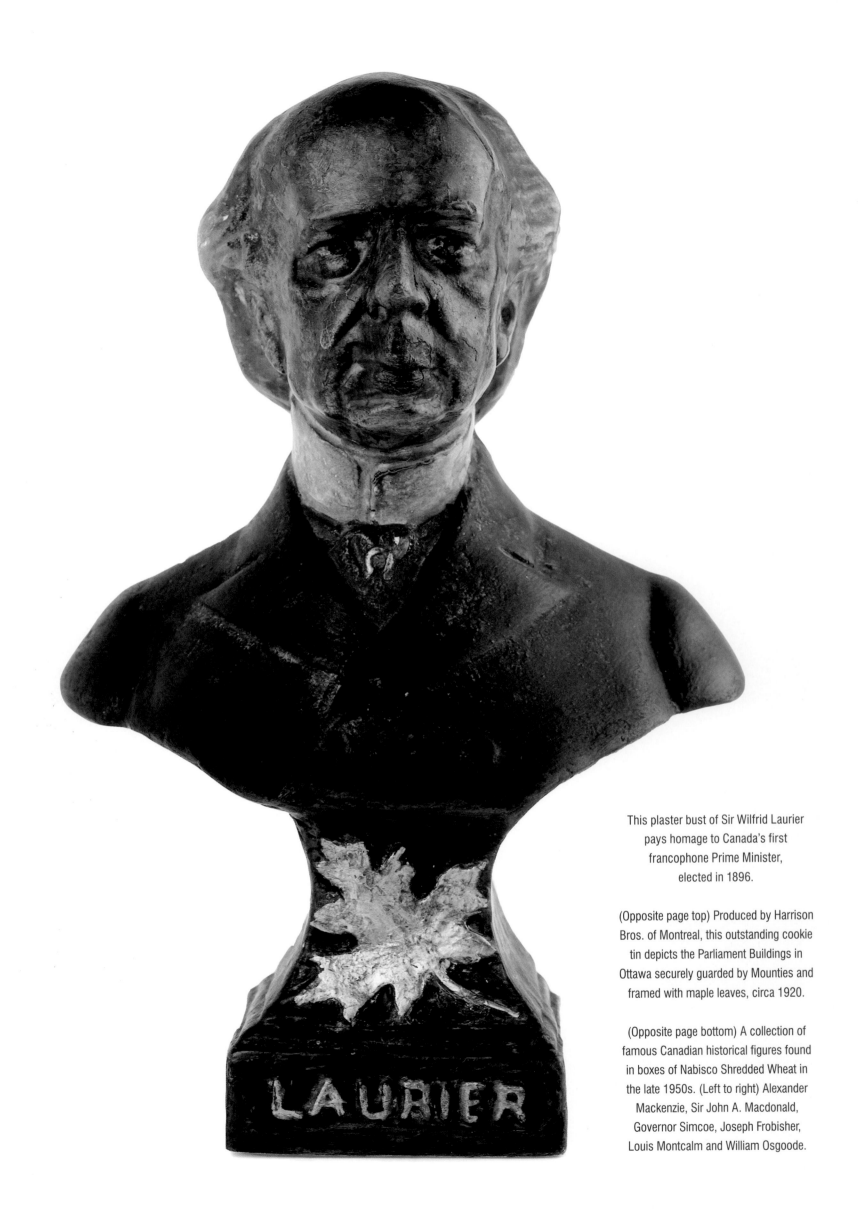

This plaster bust of Sir Wilfrid Laurier pays homage to Canada's first francophone Prime Minister, elected in 1896.

(Opposite page top) Produced by Harrison Bros. of Montreal, this outstanding cookie tin depicts the Parliament Buildings in Ottawa securely guarded by Mounties and framed with maple leaves, circa 1920.

(Opposite page bottom) A collection of famous Canadian historical figures found in boxes of Nabisco Shredded Wheat in the late 1950s. (Left to right) Alexander Mackenzie, Sir John A. Macdonald, Governor Simcoe, Joseph Frobisher, Louis Montcalm and William Osgoode.

CANADIANS A

CORONATION

A chromo-lithograph celebrating the coronation of King Edward VII in 1902, featuring a troop of
Canada's Red Coats and, in the carriage, Canada's Prime Minister, Sir Wilfrid Laurier.

(Top) This Confederation toffee tin from the 1960s shows Canada's first Prime Minister, Sir John A. Macdonald. It was produced by Gray Dunn Biscuit Manufacturers, Scotland.

(Bottom left) A commemorative Wedgwood cup with the Dominion of Canada crest, made in England circa 1900.

(Bottom right) Dominion of Canada commemorative plate, made in Austria circa 1900.

(Opposite page) This commemorative image celebrates the reign of Queen Victoria (1837-97). Note that our beloved beaver pays homage as an emissary from Canada.

HER MAJESTY THE QUEEN
1837-1887.

York, 1794.   Toronto, 1834.

Canada   **our Home**

TORONTO OF OLD

York Pioneers
AND HISTORICAL
Society

ESTABLISHED THE TORONTO 1869

Incorporated 1890.

This is to Certify

That *John Walton*

Of *The City of Toronto, Co. of York, Province of Ontario.*

Born in the county of Armagh, Ireland 22nd Sept 1836.

Settled in Toronto in 1847.

Became a Member of **York Pioneers' Society**

On the 9th day of January 1890.

OBT.

Henry Scadding, D. D.
PRESIDENT

Robert Playter, Secy.
SECT

Designed & Lithographed By Rolph, Smith & Co. Toronto, Ont.

(Opposite page) The town of York became the city of Toronto in 1834. This certificate from the York Pioneers and Historical Society was presented to A. John Malloy in 1890. An Irish immigrant, Malloy came to Canada and settled in Toronto in 1847. Collection of Black Creek Pioneer Village.

(Top) A candy tin produced by Gray Dunn Biscuit Manufacturers, Scotland, to celebrate Canada's Centennial in 1967.

(Bottom) Two colourful expressions of Canada's heritage. On the left, the Canadian and provincial coats of arms. On the right, an outstanding folk-art cushion celebrating King George's Silver Jubilee in 1935. Note that the beaver and maple leaf supersede the Union Jack and Red Ensign.

The Canadian Exp

"From the Land of the Maple Leaf" pays homage to the Canadian Expeditionary Force, whose motto was "Either Conquer or Die." The tin was made by Christie, Brown & Company Ltd., Toronto & Montreal, 1915.

(Opposite page) A collection of Canadian medals and pins from various Canadian regiments and institutions, and incorporating maple leaves and beavers. Top row (left to right): Fort Garry Horse; Canadian Garrison Regiment; Bank of Montreal medallion; Canadian Pioneer Battalion. Second row: Leeds and Grenville Battalion; Canadian Ordnance Corps; Canadian Engineers. Third row: 33rd Infantry Battalion of London, Ontario, July 1, 1915; 35th Infantry Battalion of Toronto, July 1, 1915; Fourth row: Niagara Rangers; Canadian Army Pays Corps, organized August 16, 1914; Arms Service Corps; The Kent Regiment. Bottom row: General Listing; General Listing, Toronto Light Infantry; Manitoba Beavers.

(Above) A dinner menu stand from the mess of the 208th Infantry "Canadian Irish" Battalion, raised and mobilized in Toronto, July 15, 1916.

These "Served at the Front" presentation
plaques were given to members of the
Canadian Expeditionary Forces who
served during the First World War.

Chocolate for our soldiers, a delectable reminder of home for those who served our country in the First World War. This chocolate tin was made by McDonald & Co., Montreal. Many veterans of World War I retell the poignant story of the first Christmas Eve in the trenches. The sounds of German soldiers singing "Silent Night" filled the air and led the Allied troops to join in. Eventually soldiers from both sides emerged from the trenches to trade chocolates, cigarettes and brandy. The young men even played a game of soccer, which was won by the Germans 3-2. On Boxing Day, both sides sadly returned to the bloody business of war. The following Christmas, the short reprieve from the ugliness was not repeated. Bitterness and battle fatigue made any pretense of celebration impossible.

KEEP
ALL CANADIANS
BUSY

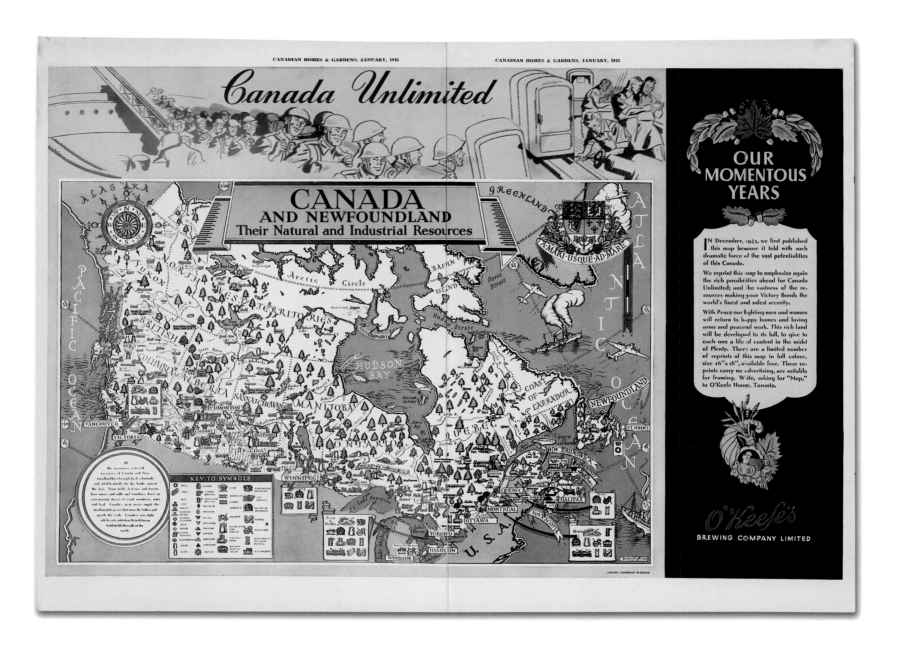

(Opposite page) Canadians were encouraged to be "busy as beavers" to ensure victory in the Great War, 1914-1918.

(Top) One of Canada's main breweries joined the war effort by encouraging Canadians and Newfoundlanders to celebrate the wealth and potential of this great land. Originally the Victoria Brewing Company (Toronto), the O'Keefe Brewery was the largest brewer in Canada during the Victorian period. During and after the prohibition, its owner, E.P. Taylor, bought out many of Canada's smaller breweries. In 1989 Molson Breweries united with Carling O'Keefe to control over half of Canadian beer manufacturing.

(Right) Patriotic Canadians proudly wore the Victory Bond pin to show their support for our troops in the "war to end all wars."

(Bottom) Invest in Canada pin, 1919.

(Top left) This hand-embroidered pillow cover honours
the brave women who participated in Canada's war effort.

(Top right) Order of St. Andrew medal, 1918-1968.

(Bottom) A Fenian Raid medal from the Ontario Rifle
Association, circa 1867-68.

Join the Team!

This poster by illustrator Ted Harris was reproduced for the 75th anniversary of the Royal Canadian Air Force by 17 Wing, Heritage. King George V introduced the prefix "Royal" for the Canadian Air Force in 1923, although April 1, 1924, became the official birthdate of the RCAF.

ROYAL CANADIAN AIR FORCE

ROYAL CANADIAN MOUNTED POLICE

1873   1973

CENTENNIAL CALENDAR

A chronological montage of Mountie uniforms from 1873 to 1973, used as the cover for the RCMP centennial calendar.

1874   1888   1897   1901   1905   1914

1915   WINTER   OFFICER   1944   OFFICER   1973

This early twentieth-century
Toronto Police helmet
employs a maple-leaf
medallion with a beaver at
the centre.

CANADA'S DIAMOND JUBILEE

A·MARI·VSQVE·AD·MARE

Armorial Bearings
of
THE
DOMINION OF CANADA

1867~1927

(Opposite page) Cover art for a 1927 program celebrating Canada's Diamond Jubilee and featuring the country's coat of arms.

(Top) This patch bears the official emblem of Canada's Centennial.

(Bottom) The Association of Chao Chow is a national organization promoting Chinese culture and education. This banner from the Montreal branch is in the collection of the Canadian Museum of Civilization.

This plaque bears the coat of arms for the city of Salaberry-de-Valleyfield, Quebec, from 1945 to 1983. The motto inscribed on the emblem, the Latin phrase *Ubi Lux Ibi Labor*, roughly translates "Light comes from work."

(Opposite page) Here is a detailed image from the "Nine Province Flag." Missing from the picture would be the Union Jack in the top left corner. This flag, which displayed Canada's early coat of arms as an addition to the Red Ensign, was used by Canadian government vessels. Originally the shield contained the arms of the four original provinces that formed the Confederation: Quebec, Ontario, New Brunswick and Nova Scotia. When Manitoba joined, the garland of maple leaves and the beaver were added around the shield. In 1907, when all provinces but Newfoundland had become members of the Dominion of Canada, the emblem on the flag was altered to contain the shields of all nine provinces.

This collage is number 42 of 200 in a series by artist James Stewart, who resided in Northern Ontario until his death in 2005. It was selected by the directors of Hamilton Place for presentation to the Right Honourable Pierre Trudeau, P.M., on the occasion of his National Unity visit to Hamilton, on November 16, 1977. The artist was extremely concerned about the state of Canadian unity.

Quebec Folk artist Claude Bolduc now resides in Geneva, Switzerland. He titled this 36" x 48" oil-on-canvas *La Mort de Meech* (1990), after the death of the Meech Lake Accord. He describes the figures as such: "On top you find Elijah Harper (the Indian with the broken clock), the Manitoban triumvirate, including their premier. Next Clyde Wells who killed the agreement with Mr. Harper. The seven remaining provincial premiers are inside the Canadian boat. Mulroney (the dragon) tears out some heads of his government (the deputies who have left his government). One of these heads is Benoit Bouchard (my cousin!). Another one is Lucien Bouchard. You find him at the end of an umbilical cord. He joined Jacques Parizeau and founded a new federal political party, 'le Bloc Quebecois.' Near Mulroney you have Jean Charest, who is the actual premier of Quebec. On the water, you find also the Quebecker's boat. Inside are two persons, Robert Bourassa and Gil Remillard. In the water you find Pierre Elliott Trudeau and Jean Chretien. The balloon up to them is the face of Frank McKenna. The Quebec is at right. It's the St-Jean Baptiste Day, the national day of Quebec. In the bottom you find some Quebec artists, Paul Piche, Gilles Vigneault, Michel Rivard and Diane Dufresne."

TRAVEL

A montage of felt souvenir pennants incorporating Mounties, maple leaves and beavers. In the prosperous decades following the Second World War, the advent of the affordable family automobile, combined with the opening of the Trans-Canada Highway, led Canadians down the road to discover their country.

April Tredgett, a former flight attendant for Trans-Canada Airlines and Air Canada, has assembled a collection of pins and souvenirs from the early days of Canadian commercial aviation history.

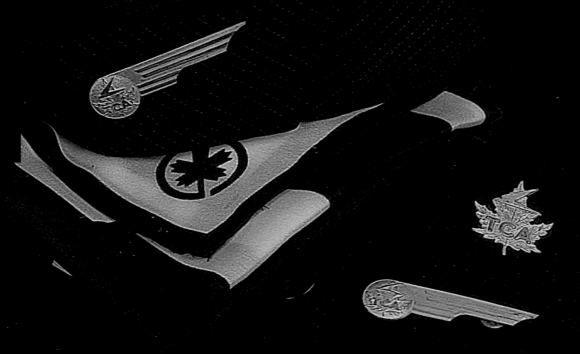

Created as a subsidiary of Canadian National Railways, Trans-Canada Air Lines launched its first flight on April 10, 1937. By 1964 TCA had grown to become Canada's national airline, and future Prime Minister Jean Chrétien introduced a private member's bill that would change the airline's name to Air Canada. Although the bill failed on first reading, it was successful on the second vote, and on January 1, 1965, Air Canada officially came into existence.

Sculptor Brian Hepburn has cleverly fashioned model airplanes from empty Canadian beer cans.

(Lower right) Two classics come together: Molson's Canadian and the legendary CF-105 Avro Arrow. Construction of the original Arrow commenced in 1953, during the height of the Cold War, in an attempt to address the threat of a Russian attack on North America by way of the North Pole. Unfortunately, the sophisticated modern interceptor was never allowed to fulfill its mission. In 1959 Prime Minister Diefenbaker's Conservative government made the still-controversial decision to cancel the Avro CF-105 and the entire Avro program.

(Upper left) Lakeport Brewing of Hamilton produces the very popular Steeler brand of beer. Mr. Hepburn fashioned an F-15 American Eagle-type fighter plane out of Steeler cans.

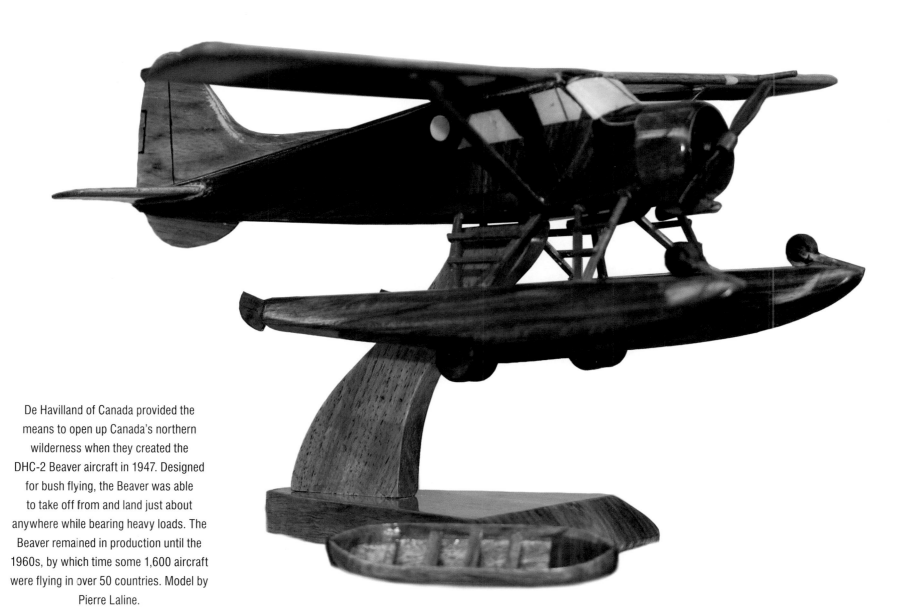

De Havilland of Canada provided the means to open up Canada's northern wilderness when they created the DHC-2 Beaver aircraft in 1947. Designed for bush flying, the Beaver was able to take off from and land just about anywhere while bearing heavy loads. The Beaver remained in production until the 1960s, by which time some 1,600 aircraft were flying in over 50 countries. Model by Pierre Laline.

the DHC·2 *Beaver*

For there was a time in this fair land when the railroad did not run When the majestic mountains alone again before man and the wheel green dark forest too silent to be real When the green dark forest was too silent to be real And many are the dead men too silent

CANADIAN NATIONAL RAILWAYS

Canadian National Railways emblem. CNR was created in 1918 as a result of a Royal Commission in 1917, at which time the Canadian government decided to combine the operations of the government-owned Canadian Government Railways and the privately owned Canadian Northern Railways System. In 1923, following difficult negotiations, CN also assumed control of the Grand Trunk Railway of Canada, which had been the oldest and largest railway system in eastern Canada. What is more evocative of the settlement of Canada than Gordon Lightfoot's " The Canadian Railroad Trilogy"

The Canadian Pacific Railway and Canadian National
Railway and their bands of steel were a force in
unifying Canada. Here, stylized diesel locomotive
4040, proudly displaying CP's beaver logo, pulls
a passenger train through the Rocky Mountains.
This logo was created by Peter Ewart in 1952. The
beaver had been part of the CPR logo since 1886.
The graphic continued to evolve until 1929, when
the beaver was taken out; only to return in 1946. It
was removed again in 1968, but following corporate
restructuring in 1996, the beaver was returned to its
lofty position as part of the company's logo.

Supertest touted itself as Canada's "All-Canadian Company." What better symbol than a maple leaf? On May 23, 1923, J. Gordon Thompson and James D. Good opened their first gasoline station in London, Ontario, under the name Supertest. By 1936 Supertest Petroleum Corporation Ltd. operated 342 stations across Ontario and Quebec. The company continued to expand their interests across Canada and was eventually sold to British Petroleum in 1971. In turn, BP was purchased by Petro Canada in 1983, at which time they elected to continue use of the Supertest name in their line of lubricants. The souvenir pump at right was made in Taiwan by Old Tyme Reproductions to a 1920 design.

SUPER DUTY

PRODUCT OF SUPERTEST SUPERTEST

GREASE

NET CONTENTS ONE POUND

"Happy Motoring": A grill medallion produced for the Royal Automobile Club of Canada.

(Right) Prior to 1995 any company could incorporate the Mountie in their advertising. In this 1930s sign, Goodrich Tires (now B.F. Goodrich of Michelin Tires) emphasizes the safety aspect of their product by displaying the trusted Mountie. Also featured here are a metal grill medallion for the Ontario Motor League, circa 1930, and a decorative porcelain grill medallion, circa 1950, made by the Dragon Manufacturing Company of France.

A desktop grouping shows the widespread use of the maple leaf, beaver and Mountie on postcards and in other stationery items.

(Top) Commemorative Canadian postage stamps from 1964.

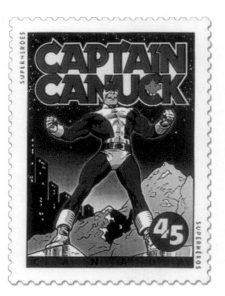

(Centre) The works of cartoonists Richard Bachle ("Johnny Canuck") and Richard Comely ("Captain Canuck") are featured in these Canadian postage stamps released in the 1990s.

(Bottom) Canada Post celebrates the 125th anniversary of the Royal Canadian Mounted Police.

The first Canadian stamp, the "Three Penny Beaver," was issued on April 23, 1851. The stamp was designed by Sir Sandford Fleming for the Province of Canada, which at the time comprised Upper and Lower Canada.

Canada's National Parks system, established in 1885, adopted the beaver for their emblem. Through the years this graphic has evolved. In the twentieth century, the use of our three major symbols became widespread and diverse.

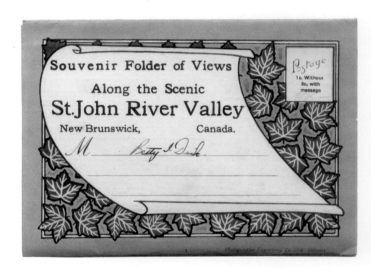

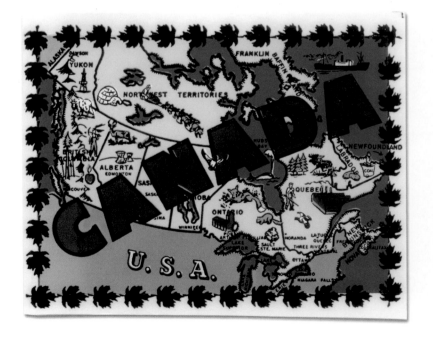

Postcards and decals proudly tell the story of a family's journeys. (Bottom left) A CPR picnic keepsake from 1894. Also displayed: a hockey medal from 1920; a 1960 medal commemorating the basketball competition in the Rome Olympics; a souvenir from the Canadian Baseball Hall of Fame and Museum in St. Mary's, Ontario; a license plate frame from Montreal, Circa 1950.

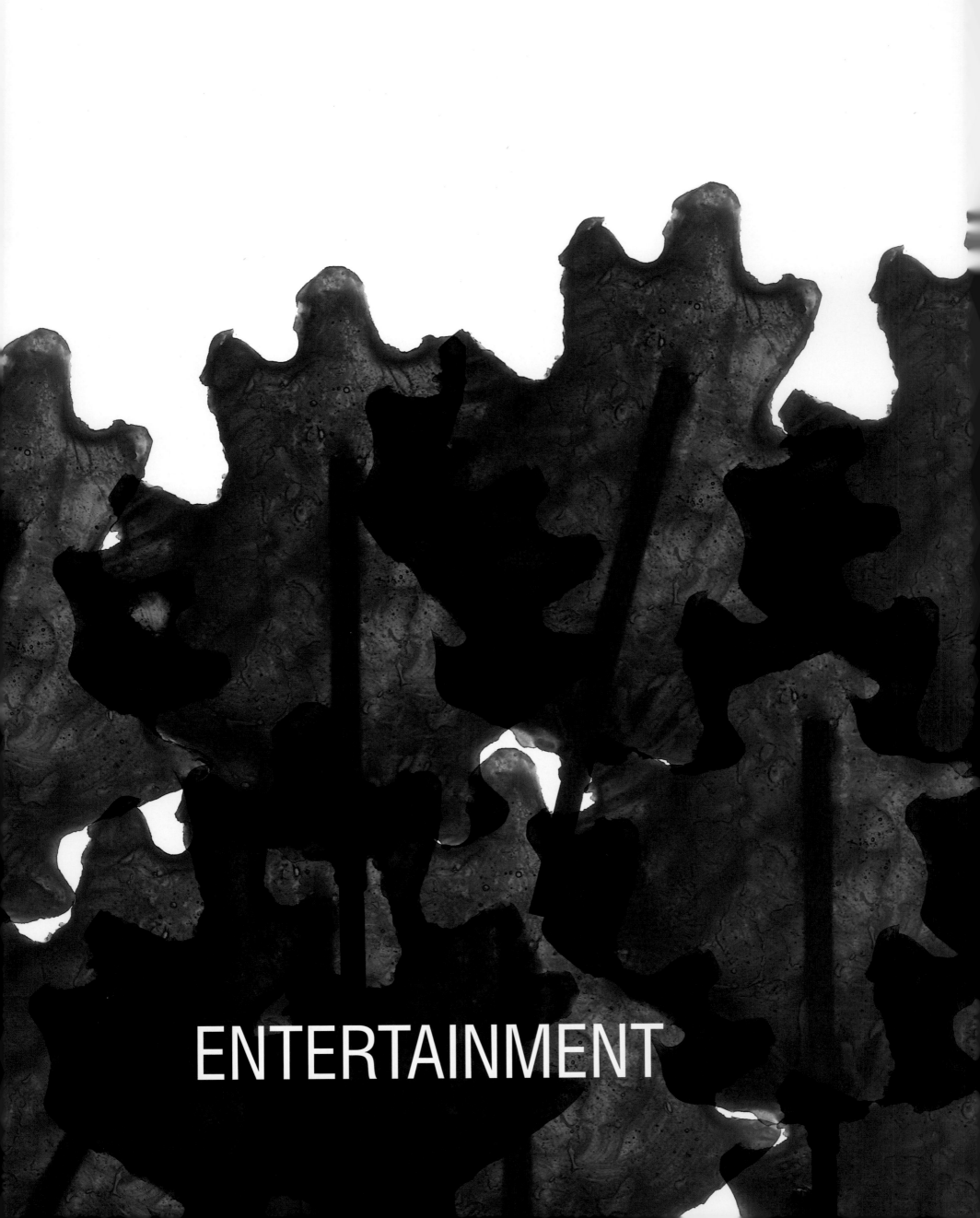

ENTERTAINMENT

Candy lollipops in a
maple-leaf design.

An assortment of smoking-related objects from the nineteenth and twentieth centuries.

(Top left) A hand-carved wooden pipe from the early twentieth century.

(Bottom left) A nineteenth-century tobacco cutter.

(Top right) A decorative and functional wooden cigarette dispenser from the early twentieth century, painted with a maple leaf and beaver. The dog's head carved at the front will fetch you a cigarette.

(Centre and bottom left) Imitation leather cigarette box and a matching tomahawk thermometer.

(Top) This Repeater Tobacco tin was manufactured for the Imperial Tobacco Co. of Canada Ltd., Montreal, circa 1916.

(Bottom) Bartholomew Houde founded his tobacco company in 1841 and helped make Quebec City a centre for that industry. In 1903 the company became a limited company, B. Houde & Company Ltee., then became part of American Tobacco Ltd. Eventually it merged with Empire Tobacco Ltd. in 1908 to form Imperial Tobacco Company of Canada. The Dominion charter under which Imperial Tobacco operates today was incorporated in 1912.

(Top) The flint lighter, embellished with the Canadian Red Ensign, was made by Auer of Japan circa 1950.

(Bottom left) T&B was the trademark of Tuckett Tobacco in Hamilton, Ontario. In 1857 George E. Tuckett opened a small shop in Hamilton, selling cigars and plug tobaccos. Tuckett continued to expand his operations until 1930, when he sold to Imperial Tobacco.

(Bottom right) A point-of-purchase display sign for Canadian Club Cigars, circa 1950.

The maple leaf decorates this wooden cigar box manufactured by John Taylor of Toronto in the early twentieth century.

(Bottom) A Grand Trunk Pacific cigar box from the late nineteenth century. Both from the collection of the Canadian Museum of Civilization.

(Opposite page) An outstanding advertising graphic from the early twentieth century, discovered on the back of an outhouse wall in Eastern Ontario.

A fine selection of twentieth-century Canadian ashtrays. Note the profound influence of the Arts and Crafts movement on the hammered-copper piece (bottom left).

ASK FOR LA B

MAPLE

MOLSON
CANADIAN

MOLSON

UPPER CANADA
Light Lager

DAWES
CANADIAN
BlackHorse
ALE

MOLSON
CANADIAN
light

NO PRESERVATIVES
SANS AGENTS DE
CONSERVATION

MOLSON
CANADIAN
LAGER BEER

MOLSON

Cheers! for
200 years

MOLSON
CANADIAN
Lager

BIÈRE

Naturally Brewed
CANADIAN
lager beer

TORONTO WINNIPEG

MOLSON
CANADIAN

MOLSON
CANADIAN

·CIRCA 1942·

TORONTO
MAPLE
LEAFS

MOLSON EXPORT Official Sponsor

In the eighteenth century, British soldiers stationed in Canada were entitled to six pints of beer a day. Consequently, the early breweries were usually built near military posts. Here we see products from two of Canada's famous breweries. Molson's Brewery, Canada's oldest, was started by John Molson in 1786 in Quebec. His company played a major role in Canada's history with their involvement in the first steamship lines up the St. Lawrence River, the development of the railway, arts and sports. The Molson Bank, founded in 1855, became part of the Bank of Montreal in 1925. Labatt's Brewery, founded by John Kinder Labatt in 1853, grew to become one of the largest and most successful breweries in Canada. The Dawe's Canadian Black Horse Ale tap handle dates back to the 1950s. All of these items of twentieth-century beer-related paraphernalia come from the collection of Lawrence Sherk.

Barton's Canadian Mist produced this limited-edition collector's decanter in the 1950s. The authentically uniformed Mountie once held fine Canadian whiskey. The box was printed in Japan, but the whiskey was bottled in the USA for Barton Distillers of New York.

SPECIAL EXPORT

SUPER LITHIATED

ESTABLISHED 1877

...EWRYS LTD. WINNIPEG, CANA...

...AT AN... OF 45...

SOUTH BE... INDIANA, U...

...HIS BEER CONTAINS MORE THAN 2½% PROOF SPIRITS

DREWRYS DRY GINGER ALE

Manufactured only by

Drewrys Dry Ginger Ale Canada, Limited

ESTABLISHED 1877
WINNIPEG   VANCOUVER

MIN. 28 FLU. OZS.

A montage of Canadian brewery labels. The beaver and maple leaf have long been associated with Canadian beer. The Drewery brands, as well as Royal Stout and Mountain Stream, were all manufactured during the 1950s. The Springbank Brewery label dates back to 1926-1929. The Empire labels go back to the 1920s. All from the collection of Lawrence Sherk.

"A SICKS' QUALITY PRODUCT"
"XXX STOUT"

BREWED FROM ...HOICEST MATERIALS

NET CONTENTS
12 FLUID OZS.

Royal *Export* Stout

NUTRITIOUS
WHOLESOME

BREWED AND
BOTTLED BY Sicks'
REGINA BREWERY LTD.

ESTABLISHED   187...

DREWRYS
(RICE   BREW)

SPECIAL BEER

*Government charges an extra Tax when any cereal ot...
...in the Manufacture of Beer. This Brew has a re...
...which all will enjoy. A Perfect Blend of Malt and...*

...YS LIMITED WINNIPEG, CANA...

CONTENTS 12 FLUID OZS.

...AINS MORE THAN 2½% PROOF SPIRITS

MOUNTAIN ST...

SPRING BANK BREWERY

MINIMUM CONTENTS 22 FLUID OZS.

TRADE   MARK

SLEEMAN'S
SPRING BANK
BREWERY CO.
LIMITED
GUELPH
ONT.

OVER 7% PROOF SPIRITS

OLD STOCK ALE

...WRYS

...ECIAL BEER

187...

*...has a really distinctive flavor which all will enjoy.
...Blend of finest Western Canadian Malt and the choicest H...*

...ODUCED
...E BEST
...& HOPS
...URABLE

REVELSTOKE, B.C.

...NTERPRISE   BREWING CO.

DREWRYS REGINA LIMITED.   REGINA, SAS...

MIN. CONTENTS 12 FLUID OZS.

Choicest
Malt

NET CONTENTS

ELEVEN OUNCES

Selected
Hops

...NTAINS MORE THAN   2½% PROOF SP...

EMPIRE

121

EMPIRE DRY

...ALE GINGER ALE

1837 THE 1897

JUBILEE

PALE ALE

The DOMINION BREWERY CO LIMITED
REGISTERED
TORONTO. CANADA

SCORE CARD.

THE GREY MARE
From Strathallan

1897

THE Jubilee Stone.

ROBT DAVIES MANAGER

WM ROSS SECRETARY.

COMPLIMENTS OF

The DOMINION BREWERY CO.

TORONTO.

Manufacturers of the

CELEBRATED

WHITE LABEL ALE.

1796.

CURLERS GREETING:

Losh man, I'm glad to see yoursel',
I'm glad to meet a freen';
But, man, the pleasure's greater still
When he's a curler keen.

But as the nicht is gye weel thru,
Drink hearty man and hale,
An drink success to ilka man,
In guid 'White Label Ale.'

CHORUS
Sae gie's the curlers grip, my freen';
Sae gie's the curlers grip
Losh man, I'm glad to see yoursel',
Sae gie's the curlers grip.

123

1896.

(Opposite page) Dominion Brewery, located on Queen Street in Toronto, was built by Robert Davies in 1878. They continued to brew until 1936, when they became one of the acquisitions of E.P. Taylor's beer empire. Dominion celebrated Queen Victoria's Diamond Jubilee with this commemorative tumbler.

This curling scorecard was produced by the Dominion Brewery Company in 1897.

A CPR bottle opener.

A beer tray from the Hamilton Brewing Association of Hamilton, Ontario, circa 1910. Note the catchy title "Regal - Spell it Backwards."

A LAUGHING...SINGING
DAREDEVIL OF THE NORTH WOODS
Renfrew
OF THE
ROYAL MOUNTED
JAMES NEWELL
CAROL HUGHS
WITH THE WONDER DOG
"LIGHTNING"
RELEASED BY SCREENCRAFT PICTURES Inc.

(Opposite page) Early Hollywood helped popularize the Canadian Mountie worldwide as a courageous and kindly hero. *Renfrew of the Royal Mounted* was a 1937 feature film based on the radio character of the same name. It was made by Grand National, directed by Albert Herman, and starred James Newell and Carolyn Hughs. Grand National went bankrupt two years later, but the Renfrew series was picked up by Monogram, and a total of eight movies were ultimately released.

Canadian actor Paul Gross continued the Mountie legacy with his portrayal of Constable Benton Fraser in *Due South*. This 1994-1996 television series was produced by Alliance Atlantis.

Coffee mugs featuring the slogan "Wild and Beautiful, I am Canadian" were produced for Swiss-Master Chocolatier of Toronto and given to guests and crew as a memento of Conan's show.

An American Mountie? In February 2004, while Toronto was still reeling economically from the devastation of the SARS crisis, a charming American came to rescue the city from its depression. Conan O'Brien brought his NBC late-night talk show to Toronto for a riotous week of entertainment and helped bring the spirit back into the city. Photo courtesy of CHUM Television, a division of CHUM Limited.

The designer of this poster adds a Canadian flair to the illustration in order to publicize the Canadian Ukrainian Music festival of 1939.

The very popular magazine *Picturesque Canada* was published from 1882-1884 by George Monro Grant. Mr. Grant, who inspired Queen's University's rise to prominence among educational institutions, was fascinated with Canada's land and culture.

Album cover and vintage vinyl for the Evaporators *I Gotta Rash*, Nard Wuar Records, Vancouver, British Columbia. Album photo by William R. Jans.

The original film *Rose Marie*, starring Nelson Eddy as the Mountie hero and Jeanette MacDonald as his love interest, is a well-known treasure. This lesser-known 1954 remake in Cinemascope by MGM, with another all-star cast, perpetuates Hollywood's ongoing fascination with the Royal Canadian Mounted Police. The choice of Mountie uniform is questionable.

(Opposite page) A wide selection of souvenir pocket knives depicting Mounties. Most of these knives were manufactured either in Germany or in Sheffield, England.

(Top) A Sheffield-made knife with a rodeo illustration celebrating the Calgary Stampede.

(Right) This fishing knife was made and packaged in England by Richards of Sheffield for export to the Canadian market.

RODEO
Canada

FISHMASTER
KNIFE

RICHARDS
OF SHEFFIELD

• LARGE KEEN BLADE
• FISH SCALER
• HOOK REMOVER
• BOTTLE OPENER

PRICE

COUTEAU de PÊCHEUR

• GROSSE LAME COUPANTE
• ÉCAILLEUR
• ENLÈVE – HAMEÇON
• OUVRE – BOUTEILLE

R·C·M·P
Canada

Printed in England

74731

MADE IN **SHEFFIELD** ENGLAND

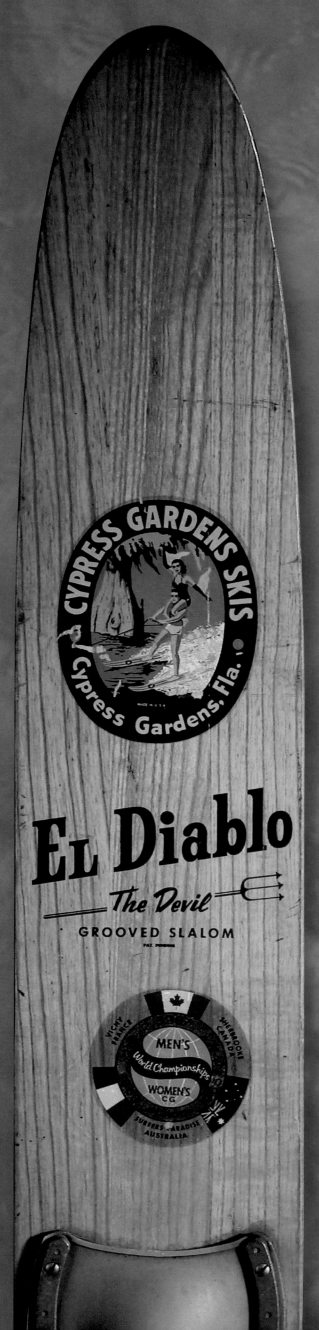

Cypress Gardens Skis commemorated the 1966 to 1968 world championships in men's and women's slalom events in a special logo on their El Diablo model water-skis. The new Canadian flag was proudly displayed alongside those of France and Australia. The 1967 competition was held in Sherbrooke, Quebec.

Kevin Harris of Vancouver was the first Canadian to become part of the elite Powell Peralta Skateboard team in California (1988). His trademark logo was designed by artist Vincent Court Johnson. Johnson managed to combine our three major symbols while still incorporating the spirit of the Bones Brigade, the team with which Kevin was affiliated.

This colourful toffee tin celebrates
a broad spectrum of Canadian
outdoor life. It was made for "the
World's Premier Toffee" company,
Thorne's from Leeds, England.

Established in 1973 with a small store in Toronto selling natural footwear, Roots now has 120 stores across North America and another 20 in Asia. Their beaver trademark has evolved through the years, as has their merchandising. A private company, Roots is famous worldwide for its quality clothing and accessories.

This Sleeman Brewery ad proudly celebrates the historic victory of its Maple Leafs baseball team, who won the first World Title Championship, in Watertown, New York, in 1874. The Sleeman family began the business of brewing when John Sleeman, from Cornwall, England, opened up the first Sleeman brewery, in Guleph, in 1851. By the turn of the century they had developed their distinctive clear bottle with the beaver emblem, a version which is still in use today.

Canada has a long and distinguished baseball history. Over a century later, in 1992, the Canadian Baseball Hall of Fame commemorated another Canadian team's historic victory, the Toronto Blue Jays' defeat of the Atlanta Braves in six games to become the first Canadian team to win the World Series.

In their long tradition of sports sponsorships, Labatt Breweries played an integral role in bringing the Blue Jays to Toronto in 1977.

(Opposite page) Vancouver artist Jeremie White painted nine 5" x 7" acrylics on canvas to create this work entitled *Goal of the Century — Canada vs. CCCP*. This moment in Canadian history took place on September 28, 1972, when two international rivals, Russia and Canada, took to the ice to determine supremacy in the world of hockey. After eight nail-biting games, Paul Henderson became a national hero when he scored the winning goal — "the goal heard around the world" — and made Canada the world champions.

(Above) A Toronto Maple Leafs doll in vintage clothing, made in Canada by Allied Co., 1962.

As Canada's national winter sport, hockey is played on streets, ponds and rinks across the country. People from all walks of life are bound together by this sport's traditions. The historic French-English rivalry has always been most joyfully celebrated when the Montreal Canadiens and the Toronto Maple Leafs meet on the ice. These metal figures were made by Eagle Toys of Montreal circa 1950 for a table-top hockey game.

HE SHOOTS

HE SHOOTS

HE SCORES!

"He shoots. He scores!" Hockey fans will always cherish these words made legendary by broadcaster Foster Hewitt.

From bubblegum cards to gasoline promotions, Canadians love their hockey heroes.
Esso came up with a novel promotional item for the 1966-67 season: "Maple Leaf
Hockey Talks," a series of recordings featuring stories and advice from legendary Leafs.
Obviously the exposure helped: they won the 1967 Stanley Cup.

Oh, the good old hockey game, is the best game you can name And the best ... can name ... d old hocke ... h, the good ... game, is th ... you can n ... e best game you can name, is ... old hockey ...

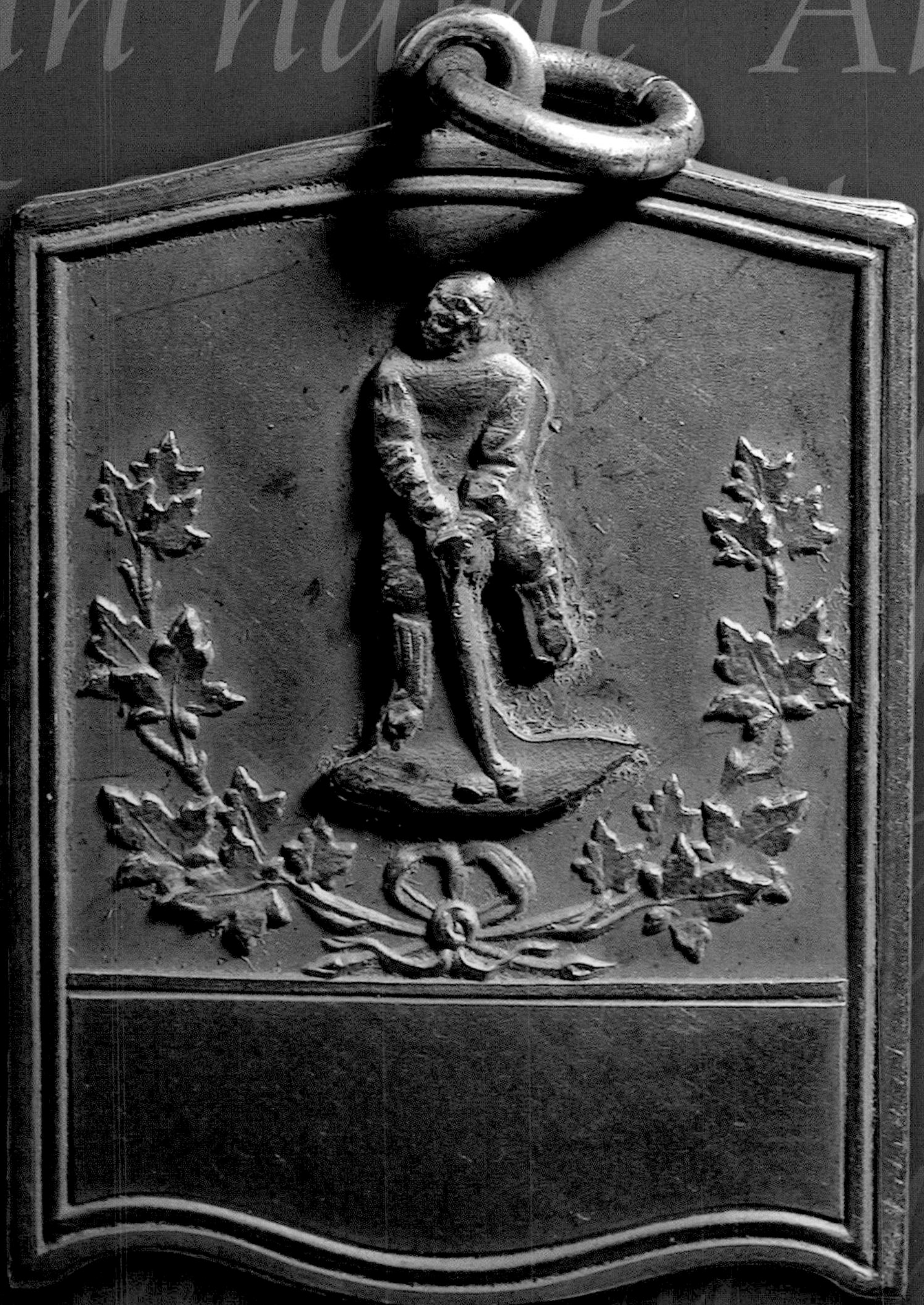

(Above) A brass hockey medallion from 1915, featuring a hockey player framed by a garland of maple leaves.

(In background) The chorus from a perennial Canadian favourite, "The Hockey Song," by Stompin' Tom Connors, 1973.

The Toronto Canadian National
Exhibition has long been a summer
destination of choice for tourists
and locals alike. Held in the last
two weeks of August, the annual
fair denotes the end of summer
and a return to school. The
designer created a memorable
logo for participants in this 1960
gymnastic clinic.

This woolen athletic shirt was worn by a member of the Sudbury Canoe Club circa 1935.

(Top, left to right) A tiny rubber Mountie doll; a small metal Mountie, circa 1950; a metal Mountie on horseback; a small lead Mountie.

(Bottom, left to right) A patriotic nutcracker doll; a felt-uniformed Native Mountie doll on a wooden base, inscribed "I am a Rogark Doll," made in South Wales circa 1930; a cellulose Mountie in felt uniform, also circa 1930.

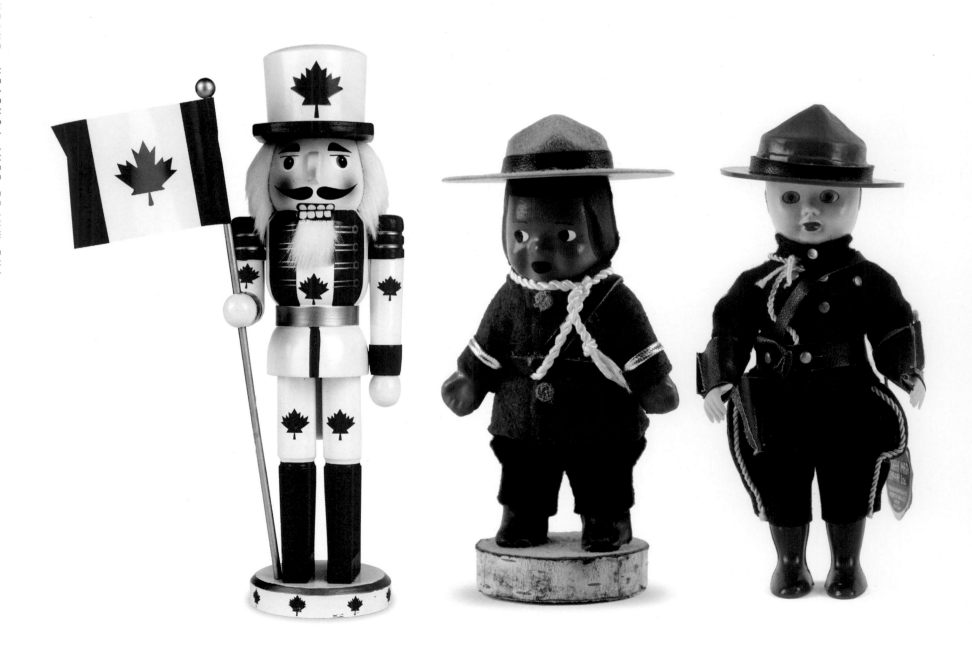

This official Mountie doll, named "John Steele," sports an authentic uniform on his 12-inch body and comes with equipment that is accurately reproduced in 1/6 scale. The copyright for this figure is held by Dragon Models Ltd. 2000, Hong Kong, but because these dolls are manufactured under license from the RCMP, every purchase supports the RCMP's community policing programs.

CANADA

A wide selection of
Mountie figures from the
1930s to the 1950s.

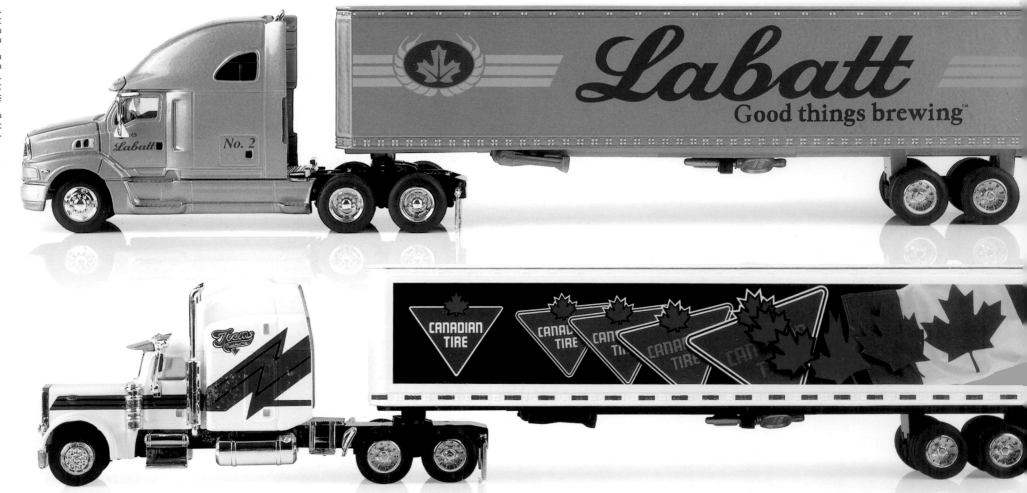

A selection of collectible toy trucks. This flotilla of trucks employs logos heralding Canada's continued use of the maple leaf and beaver in corporate imaging: Canada Cartage's logo appears on a Sterling day cab; Labatt's image is spread across a tractor trailer; Canadian Tire Corporation's colourful logo is emblazoned on this tractor trailer; the vintage 1938 Chevrolet panel truck sports the Supertest logo; Canadian Pacific's logo appears on a tractor trailer; and the Canadian Pacific logo on a 1950 Chevrolet stake truck.

An RCMP shooting game based on the late 1950s
television series *R.C.M.P.*, which was made by
Crawley Films (Ottawa) out of their Chelsea,
Quebec, studio. The game was manufactured by
A. Wells & Company Ltd., Great Britain.

PRECISION MADE
SHOOTING GAME

with endless fun!

K DOWN THE BEAR

p pops the LION

K DOWN THE LION

p pops the BEAR

R.C.M.P
SHOOTING GAME

**BASED ON THE B.C.C. T.V. SERIES
with GILLES PELLETIER as
Cpl. JACQUES GAGNIER.**

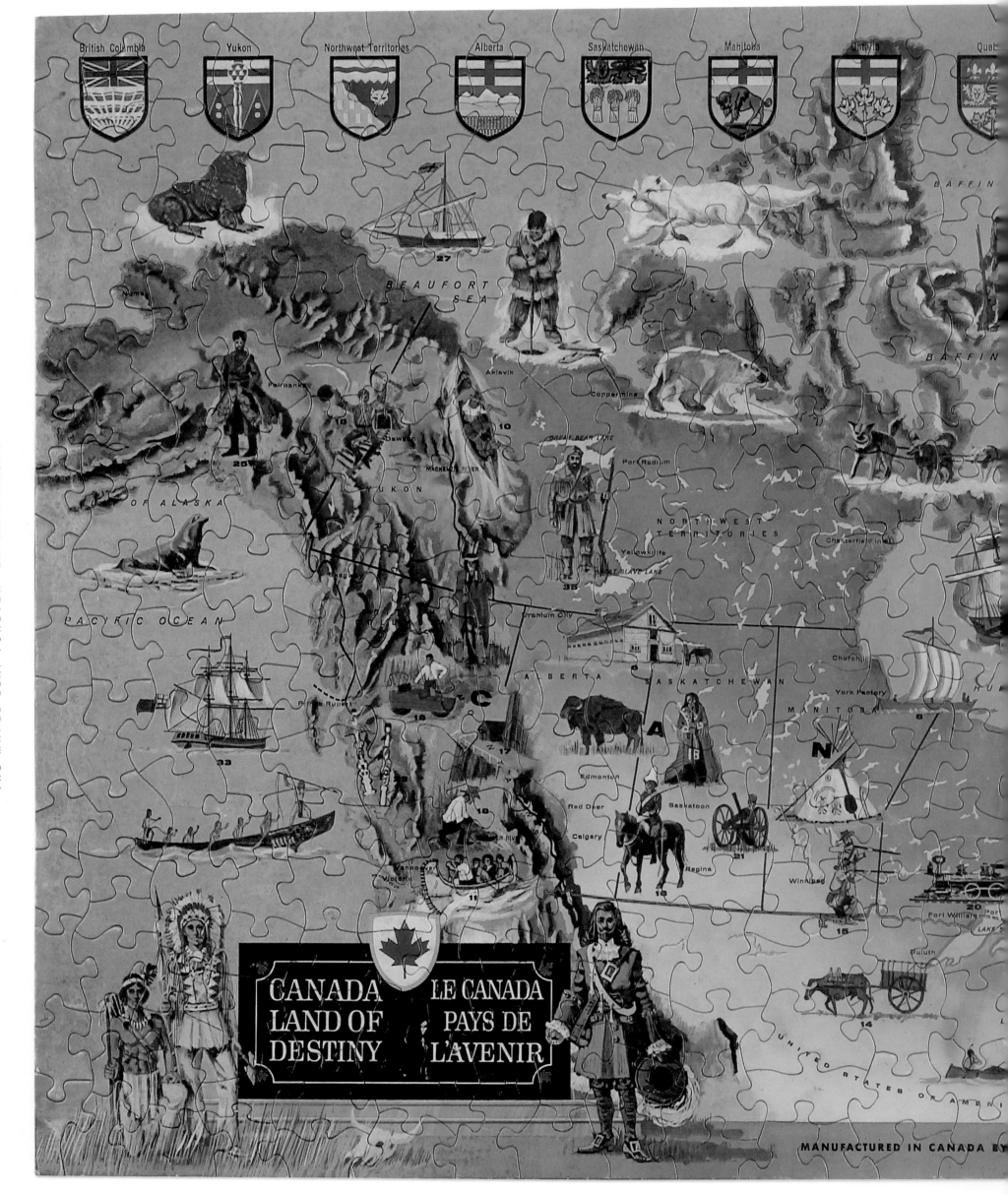

KER BROTHERS GAMES LIMITED

COPYRIGHT 1966

(Right) Hasbro-Parker Brothers created this informative and graphically delightful jigsaw puzzle portraying Canada's history. (Top) One of Petro-Canada's promotional premiums was an educational Canadian quiz book for youngsters. (Bottom) A vintage wooden jigsaw puzzle with scenes of Mounties defending the stagecoach, circa 1940.

(Left to right) An embossed leather souvenir bank from Niagara Falls; a child's beaver bank; a beer bottle bank; a "Maple Leaf" mock cash register bank manufactured by the Durable Toy Novelty Co., New York City/Cleveland; a hand-stenciled tin mailbox bank.

A Canada colouring book with a Mountie and his faithful dog on cover, circa 1950.

THE MAPLE LEAF FOREVER ENTERTAINMENT

A Classics Illustrated comic from June 1959. Superintendent J.C. Story, RCMP (retired), was a consultant for this special issue.

Richard Comely's comic-book superhero, Captain Canuck, may not enjoy the celebrity of his many American counterparts, but he is a legend in Canadian popular culture. Comely was only 24 when the first issue of *Captain Canuck* appeared in 1975. The original artwork for the first 14 issues, as well as an unpublished Issue 15, was acquired by the Canadian National Archives in 1992. Comely still hopes that his non-brooding patriotic superhero will one day make a comeback, and in that regard he is presently in negotiations to create a new television series.

AT HOME

Detail from a hand-carved wooden panel. The artist, Jean-Baptiste Cote (1832-1907), of Quebec, trained as an architect but chose instead to pursue a career as a woodcarver in Quebec's shipbuilding industry.

(Top) A doorknocker from the early twentieth century that features a patinated cast beaver on a maple leaf field.

(Bottom) A cast-iron decorative wall-hanging from the late nineteenth century.

Hand-carved wooden trencher found
in Eastern Ontario and dating to the
mid-nineteenth century. During the
long, dark winter nights, without the
distractions of modern inventions, the
early settlers honed their creative skills
and applied them to their domestic
creations. Treen (or woodenware),
ironware, quilts, blankets and rugs
became works of art as well as
utilitarian objects for household use.

(Top left) A handmade hooked mat from Quebec, circa mid-nineteenth century. (Bottom left) Another handmade hooked mat, this one fash oned by a New Brunswick artist to celebrating Canada's Centennial in 1967. (Bottom centre) As one of Canada's cherished symbols, the beaver has always been a popular subject for hooking. (Top right) A colourful and humorous twentieth-century hooked mat from Ontario. (Bottom right) This Barrymore Confederation Rug was made by the Toronto Carpet Manufacturing Company Ltd., which has been making carpets since 1891.

Long before washing machines were invented, women of the household
were as "busy as beavers" scrubbing the laundry on their washboards.
Circa 1920.

Notice the beaver detailing in this fine sewing machine. Raymond Sewing Machines were first created in 1862 by American Charles Raymond. He moved his operations from Vermont to Guelph, Ontario, to avoid lawsuits initiated by the Singer Company, whose machines he had copied. During the Civil War the demand for uniforms and other items of clothing led to a boom in sewing machine sales. In 1916 the White Sewing Machine Company acquired Raymond Manufacturing and moved the factory to its Cleveland facility. This machine is from the collection of Black Creek Pioneer Village.

(Top) Needles were safely stored in this colourful package from the early twentieth century.

(Centre) This tape measure with Mountie and maple leaf was made in Germany circa 1950.

(Bottom) These hand-forged sewing shears were found in upstate New York. Note the tiny beavers incised on the upper blade, circa 1800.

A collection of Furnival china celebrating Canadian scenes and symbols. T. Furnival & Sons was established in 1851 and produced china under the name Furnivals until 1913, when the name was changed to "Furnivals (1913) Ltd." In 1968 the works were closed, and the trademark name now belongs to Josiah Wedgwood & Sons Ltd.

A collection of souvenir plates. (Top left) A plate bearing the coat of arms of the Dominion of Canada, maker unknown. (Centre left) Made in England by Wedgwood circa 1900 and featuring the nine-province coat of arms. (Bottom left) Canada-US friendship plate made by Royal Winton, Grimwades, England. (Centre) This beautiful hand-painted plate is titled "The Maple Leaf Forever" and was made in England. (Top right) This plate displaying the floral emblems of Canada was manufactured for Coast Craft by Royal Winton of England. (Centre right) With the approval of the commissioner, this plate was manufactured by Spode of England to commemorate the centenary of the RCMP. Plate # 741 of 2,000. (Bottom right) This decorative plate featuring the ten provinces was painted in Canada.

(Top) This Mountie plate features "Bill McMillan '84." Stamped AK Kaiser, West Germany, the plate was decorated in Canada.

(Bottom) Mountie plate, made in Japan.

THE ROYAL CANADIAN MOUNTED POLICE

(Left and below) Hand-painted ashtray and teapot set, made in Japan.

(Right) Beaver salt-and-pepper shakers.

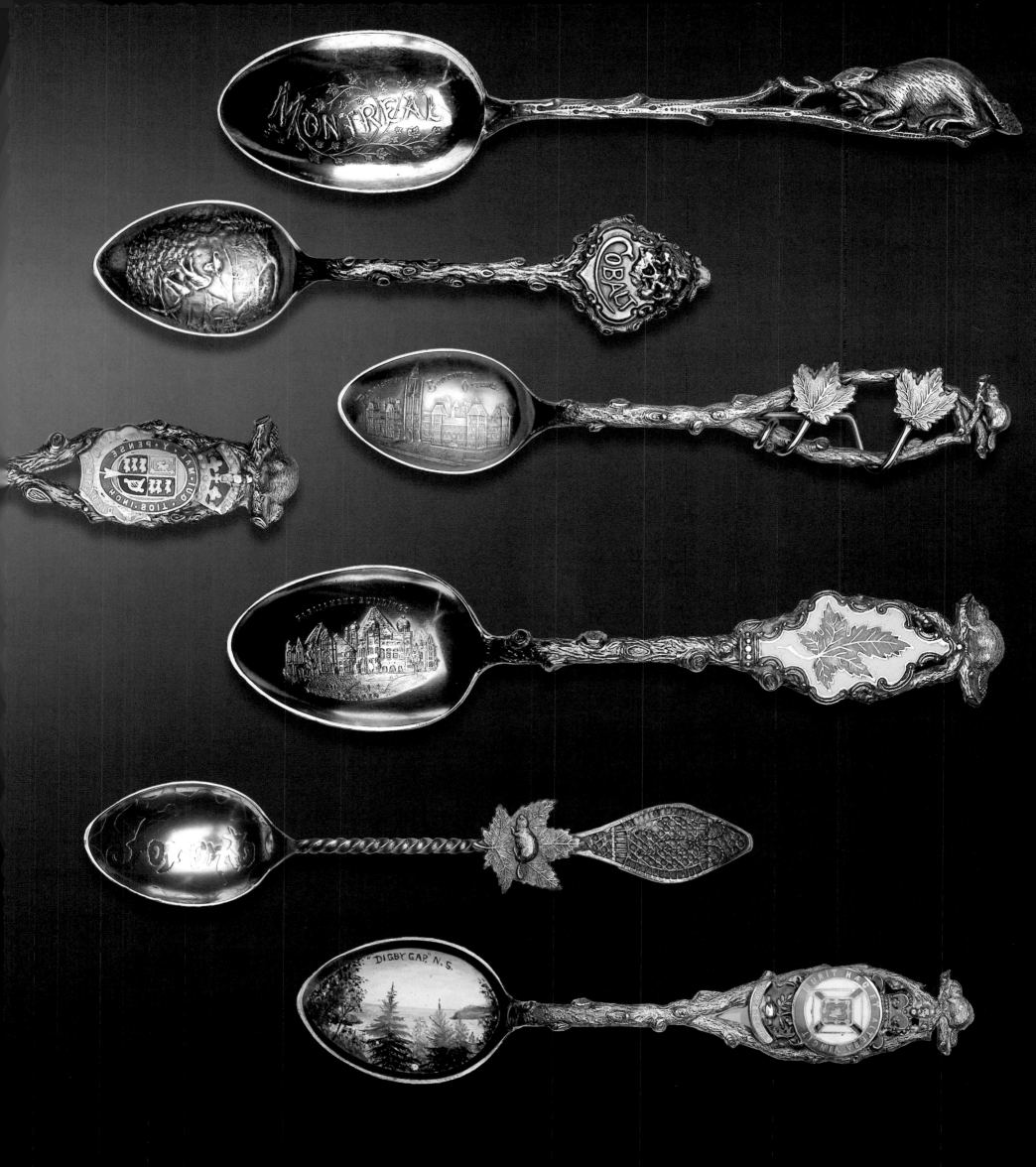

An outstanding collection of Canadian souvenir spoons from various towns, sporting events and festivals, featuring beavers and maple leaves.

A collection of handmade and manufactured bottles and jars, each employing beaver or maple leaf motifs, dated from the mid-1900s to the early twentieth century. By 1839 United Empire Loyalist Nathaniel Mallory had the first recorded glass house in Canada, in the village of Mallorytown, near Brockville, Ontario. By 1865 Hamilton had the Hamilton Glass Works, and other cities began to follow with their own companies. Most early Canadian glass works were built near suitable sources of sand or on shipping routes so that sand and other raw materials could be readily transported to their factories.

This amber beaver sealer, with the beaver facing right, was manufactured at the Ontario Glass Company in Kingsville, Ontario, in the late nineteenth century. An amber beaver sealer with a left-facing beaver is a rare and highly collectible item and was probably produced by Diamond Glass Company in the late nineteenth century.

A Canadian pressed-glass cake plate with maple leaf motif. Four
Canadian glass companies produced pressed glass: Burlington
Glass, Nova Scotia Glass, Jefferson Glass (the Toronto division
of the US company) and Dominion Glass, which overtook the
other three in 1913. Maple leaf-patterned glass is thought to be
solely Canadian and was produced by two companies, Diamond
Glass of Montreal and later Jefferson Glass of Toronto.

Canadian pressed-glass goblets and bowls in the maple-leaf style. Most glassware was not marked by the manufacturer and therefore it is difficult to identify the source. These are from the early twentieth century.

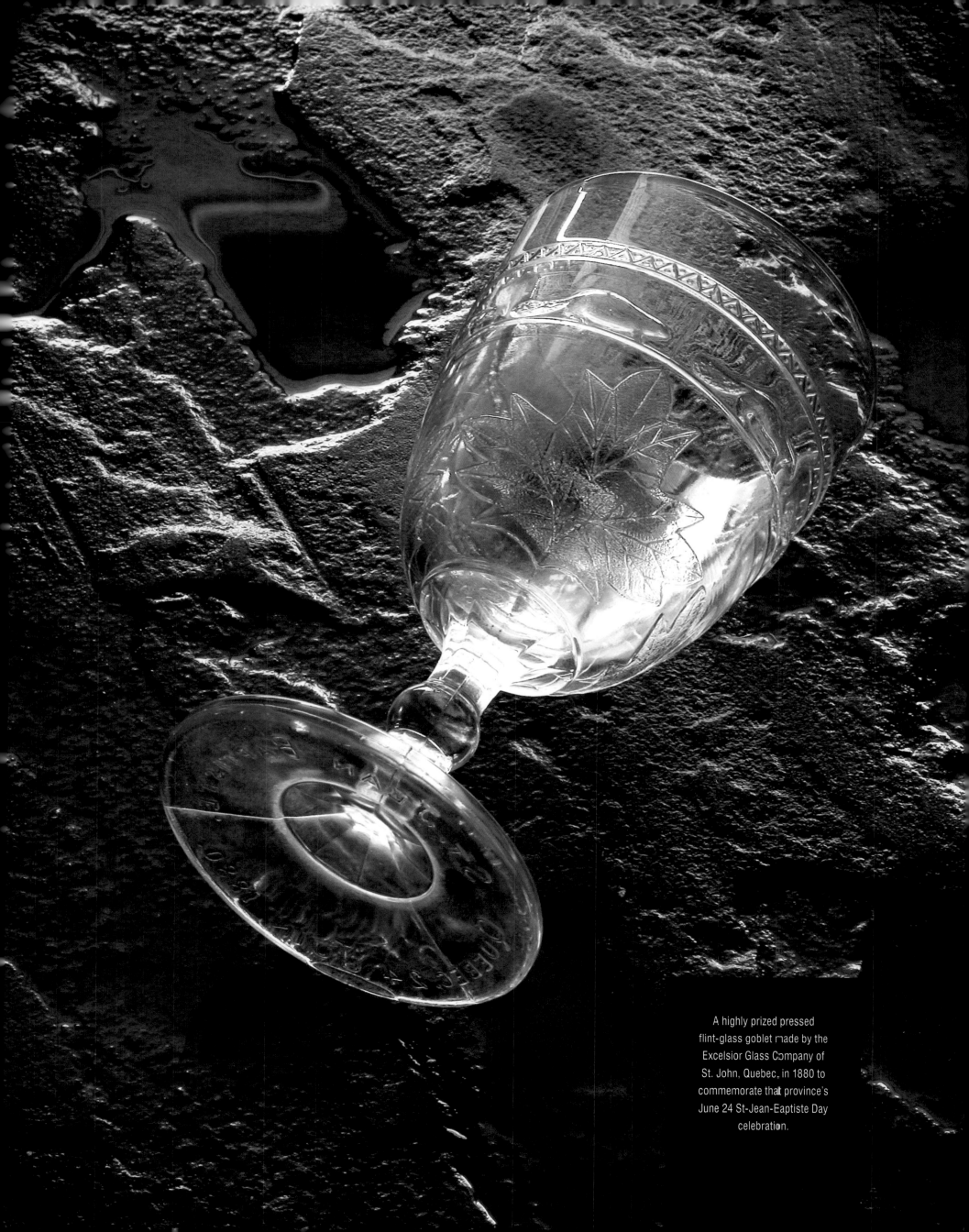

A highly prized pressed
flint-glass goblet made by the
Excelsior Glass Company of
St. John, Quebec, in 1880 to
commemorate that province's
June 24 St-Jean-Eaptiste Day
celebration.

An assortment of souvenirs and memorabilia. (Bottom right) The delicate hand-painted beaver paperweight at bottom right was made in England in 2001 by Royal Crown Derby. Titled the "Riverbank Beaver," this particular item, from a private collection, is #1505 of 5,000.

(Top left) A cast-iron picture frame stamped "R.D. 1929." (Top centre) One of a pair of cast-bronze bookends, circa 1920. (Bottom left) An embossed leather photo album, circa 1930. (Right) A cast-iron "Jenny Lind" Federal-style mirror from the mid-nineteenth century.

An assortment of jewelry with
a distinctively Canadian flair,
dating from the mid-nineteenth
century to the present.

Early twentieth-century studio photograph of an unknown Mountie, from the G.H. Wheeler studio in Sydney, Cape Breton.

G.H. Wheeler
SYDNEY. C. B.

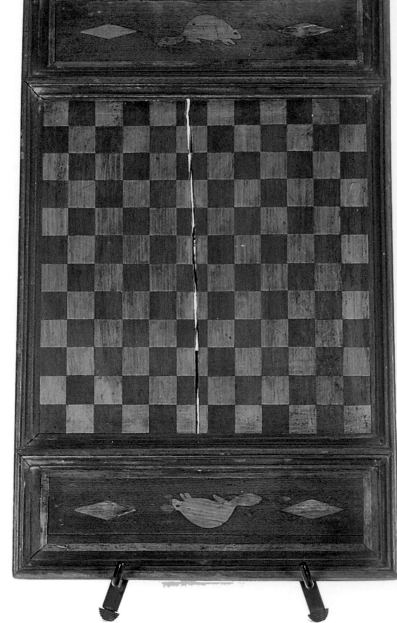

(Above) This outstanding Victorian tilt-top table
is truly a work of art. The table's central panel
was painted by Cornelius Kreighoff. The garland
that surrounds the painting is made up of real
maple leaves collaged onto the surface. Titled
"Portage at Grand D'Mere Falls," it is now part of
the Collection of the Royal Ontario Museum.

(Right) A charming and decorative games board
from the mid-nineteenth century.

A St. Laurent-style woodstove door
from Quebec, circa 1877.

This ashtray holder from the mid-twentieth century shows modern international styling with a Canadian touch, circa 1950.

A glorious late-nineteenth-
century rocking chair from
Quebec employing maple
leaves and beaver motifs in its
pressed-wood back.

ARTISTIC EXPRESSION

Detail of the Mountie Quilt created by Beth Craig in 1975, now in the collection of the Canadian Museum of Civilization.

Carved wooden Mountie in the
naïve tradition, found in Etobicoke,
Ontario, circa 1940.

(Right) A Ukrainian Easter egg painted in 1972 by a Mrs. Baczynka of Montreal. (Left) A hand-painted goose-egg shell from the Polish community, found in La Salle, Quebec. Both are in the collection of the Canadian Museum of Civilization.

A folk-art hooked mat found
in Polar Point, Manitoba,
celebrates Canadian pride,
circa 1930.

This child-size woolen sweater featuring the maple leaf was hand-knitted in the mid-twentieth century and is in the collection of the Canadian Museum of Civilization.

CANADA
1917

Members of Native tribes would often trade beaver pelts for colourful glass beads from Europe. Beading became an art form and was used to create magnificent ceremonial and decorative pieces. Each tribe's work could be readily distinguished by its particular use of colours and motifs.

(Left) A beaded heart-shaped cushion made in the Native tradition. (Centre) A late-nineteenth-century hand-carved wooden West Coast Aboriginal canoe paddle. Note the beaver on the blade. (Top right) Handmade beadwork in the Native tradition, found near Goderich, Ontario, and celebrating Canada's centennial. (Bottom right) A colourful early twentieth-century Aboriginal quill box in the tradition of the Woodland tribes of southwestern Ontario.

An Aboriginal quill box
featuring the maple leaf motif,
circa 1950.

Portrait of Madonna and child. The gold maple-leaf symbol is repeated on the female image and on the child, with the fleurs-de-lis in the centre. This work by Slavko Protic, a Serbian artist from British Columbia, is entitled *Mother of God of Canada* and is in the collection of the Canadian Museum of Civilization.

The oil painting *A Prairie Fire* by Calgary's Christian N. Frey, from the collection of the Canadian Museum of Civilization.

Sergeant — North-West Mounted Police 1874   Sergent — Police à cheval du Nord-Ouest 1874

Sergeant — North-West Mounted Police 1898   Sergent — Police à cheval du Nord-Ouest 1898

Sergeant — Royal Canadian Mounted Police 1979   Sergent — Gendarmerie royale du Canada 1979

As part of Toronto's centenary celebration, artist Thomas McNeely was commissioned by the RCMP to create these illustrations. Each figure is representative of a real Mountie. Mr. McNeely's neighbours became curious when Mounties began appearing on his doorstep in full dress uniform to model for this series.

Artist Diane Durrand was commissioned by Canada Place to create sculptures for the 1986 World
Exposition on Transportation and Communication held in Vancouver. These sculptures were to be
representative of Canada and of Expo '86's main themes. The result was *Canada's National Shoe Set*,
a down-to-earth perspective on locomotion. The 13 sculptures consisted of carefully chosen used
footwear dipped in liquid plastic and then painted with acrylics. Ms. Durrand "fell in love with Canada
all over again" during the six months it took to complete the project. The shoes pictured here are titled
"Province of Canada" and are now in the collection of the Canadian Museum of Civilization.

Sporting a pillbox hat, this handmade wooden Mountie was used as a store sign. It was found by an antique dealer in Ontario's Muskoka Lakes region.

(Top) This delightful naïve oil-on-board painting evokes the childhood myth of the Mountie and his horse. It was found in Scarborough, Ontario, and dates to the mid-twentieth century.

(Bottom left) Folk-art beaver from the late twentieth century by a P.E.I. artist.

(Bottom right) Carved wooden Mountie, signed Hannah, circa 1950.

(Left) A handmade Mountie lawn figure from mid-twentieth century. (Top centre) The Sawyer family plaque, found in Guelph, Ontario, follows the historic tradition of incorporating maple leaf and beaver symbols in the expression of one's Canadian identity. (Bottom centre left) A late-nineteenth-century beaver weathervane from Quebec. (Bottom centre right) A whimsical figure made from Canadian beer bottle caps, found near Waterloo, Ontario, circa 1960. (Bottom right) A beaver ashtray holder created by Quebec carver C. Dube, circa 1940.

Weathervanes are a symbol of man's dependence upon the weather. The figure in a weathervane (or weathercock) sits freely on a vertical rod and is able to turn in any direction. By design, it always points into the wind or the wind always comes from the direction that the weathervane points. "Vane" comes from the old English word *fane*, meaning "flag or banner." These devices have been traced back to 48 B.C., when humans had come to recognize the relationship between wind and weather. When settlers arrived in this country, they would often fabricate figures that were symbolic of their new life in Canada. As time went on, the art form became as important as the functionality of design. The unique sculptures have become highly prized objects. These are from the collection of the Museum of Civilization.

(Top left) An early nineteenth-century blacksmith-made beaver weathervane from St. Lambert, Quebec. (Bottom left) This sheet-metal horse weathervane with maple leaf came from Pictou, Nova Scotia, late nineteenth century. (Top right) Tin weathervane, from the lower St. Lawrence area of Quebec, featuring a beaver on a maple-tree branch, late nineteenth century. (Bottom right) Metal weathervane depicting beaver on branch.

ACKNOWLEDGMENTS

It would have been impossible for us to complete this project without the support of many individuals, businesses and organizations.

Our sons, Dylan and Jesse, continually expressed their delight and enthusiasm through the many years that we spent assembling this collection.

Publisher John Denison of Boston Mills Press immediately supported the project and helped see it through to its completion. Managing editor Noel Hudson challenged the creative process and provided encouragement.

Photographer and art director Matthew Beverly infused this project with his talent and energy. He gratefully acknowledges the support of Michael Beverly; as well as his wife and his beautiful daughter, Ella Marie.

Many of the following people were tirelessly generous with time, information and access to hidden treasures. Many thanks go to Cindy Henry of the RCMP; staff at the Museum of Civilization, especially Dr. Sheldon Posen, Annie LaFlamme, Frederic Paradise, Huguette Desmarais and Martin Villeneuve; Nicola Woods at the Royal Ontario Museum; Jim Hunter and Derek Cooke of Black Creek Pioneer Village; Paul Cabot of the Toronto Aerospace Museum; Jonathan Hannah of CPR Archives; and Bronwyn Quarrie and Dorothy Bosma of the Hudson's Bay Company Archives.

Our special thanks to John and Mary Fawcett, April Tredgett, and to Marion Hebb for her patience. Our gratitude to Pandora Press; Grand Valley Fortifiers Ltd.; Locke and Mackenzie Antiques; Jim and Brenda Orton; Elvis at Comet Collectables; Art and Jean Alder; Burt Bell; Jeff Ferguson at Waddington's Auctioneers and Appraisers; Julie Heath and staff at Warner Bros.; Kevin Harris and Michael Farkahara at Powell Skateboard; Jeremie White; Kathleen Hooper; Brian Hepburn; Diane Durrand; Jack and Judy Welton; Steven Greenberg; Gerry Marks of Pollikers Antiques; Lawrence Sherk; Richard Comely; Michelle Harries and Christine Liao at Petro Canada Ltd.; Jill-Marie Burke at de Havilland-Bombardier; Suzanne Dusing at Procter & Gamble; Zela Mohamed at Maple Leaf Foods Inc.; Suzannah Riggs at Cadbury Canada; Chiara Architta at U.S. Michelin; Linda Cobon at the C.N.E.; Geoff Flint; The Blue Pump; Bill Pinkney of Pinkney's of Peel; Gino Stea at the Print In; Hamid Nasery of Fancy Frames; Glen McIlven and Roxanne Keeping at Steichenlab; Serge Shereshevsky; Air Canada; Claude Bolduc; James Stewart; Lori Ball at Molson Brewing Company; John Sleeman of Sleeman Brewery; Kathleen Murphy at Labatt Breweries; Nadine McLeod of Lakeport Brewing Corporation; Josie Camilletti at Pepsi; George and Miles Hernaez of G&Y Antiques; Colette Walker at Sears Canada Inc.; Maeve Burke at Canadian Tire Corporation; Robert Hall of Canada Cartage; Robert Sarner and Ilich Mejia at Roots; Winnie Runnquist; J.R. Skeffington of The Toy Truck Place; Ken Aubrey and Jean Murray of Aubrey's Antiques & Nostalgia; Stephanie Gonzalez at Classic Media.tv; Matthew J. Shuber of the Toronto Blue Jays; the Toronto Maple Leafs; Bill Tull and Marc Liepisz from Late Night with Conan O'Brien; LeeAnn Platner of the NBC legal department; and Christina Litz at CHUM Limited.

When we first became involved in collecting antiques and folk art, we had the good fortune at that time to be in the company of this country's most knowledgeable dealers and collectors: Drs. Murray and Mary Copeland, Phil Shackleton, and Blake and Ruth McKendry. Our contemporaries have provided lively discussions and debate, and also challenged and influenced our terms of reference. These people include the late Michael Bird, Chris Huntington, Murray Stewart, Ken and Doris Lawless, Wes & Joan Mattie, Bill Dobson, Tim and Gerda Potter, Clay and Carol Benson, Jim and Ilona Fleming, Dr. Ralph and Patricia Price, Paul Byington, Peter Baker, Michael Rowan, Howard Paine, Jim Wills, Larry Foster, John McInnis, and Jennifer McKendry.

Our thanks also to Danny Burke, Anna Gold, and Zena and Jean Paul Laroche for their support and friendship.

BIBLIOGRAPHY

BOOKS

Blachette, Jean-Francois, et al., under the direction of Pierre Crepeau. *From the Heart: Folk Art in Canada.* McClelland and Stewart Ltd., in cooperation with the Museum of Man/National Museums of Canada, Toronto, 1983.

Cameron, Jim. *The Canadian Beaver Book.* General Store Publishing House, Burnstown, Ontario, 1991.

Canadian Heritage. *Symbols of Canada.* The Department of Canadian Heritage, Canadian Government Publishing, Ottawa, 2002.

Charters, Dean. *Mountie.* Collier-Macmillan Canada Ltd., Don Mills, Ontario, 1973.

Crawford, Douglas A. *County Canners.* County Magazine Printshop Ltd., Blomfield, Ontario, 2003.

Coupland, Douglas. *Souvenir of Canada 2.* Douglas & McIntyre Ltd., Vancouver, 2004.

Dawson, Michael. *The Mountie, from Dime Novel to Disney.* Between the Lines, Toronto, 1998.

Fulford, Robert. *Canada: A Celebration.* Key Porter Books Ltd., Toronto, 1997.

Herriott, Ted. *The Canadian Heritage Label Collection.* Purpleville Publishing, Mississauga, Ontario, 1982.

Horwood, Harold. *A History of Canada.* Bison Books Corp., Conneticut, 1983.

Matheson, John Ross. *Canada's Flag: A Search for a Country.* Mika Publishing Co., Belleville, Ontario, 1986.

Stevens, Gerald. *Early Ontario Glass.* University of Toronto Press, Toronto, 1965.

Unitt, Doris and Peter. *Bottles in Canada.* Clock-House Pub., Peterborough, Ontario, 1972.

WEBSITES

www.atlasgeo.net/fotw/flags/ca-9prov.html

www.canadianheritage.gc.ca/newsroom/index

www.cbc.ca/50tracks/essentialcanadianmusic.html

www.collections.ic.gc.ca/clan/clans/beaverclan.htm

www.info.detnews.com/history/story/index

www.firstpeople.us/FP-HTml-Legends

www.humanities.mcmaster.ca/~pjohnson/home.html

www.pch.gc.ca/progs/cpsc-ccsp/sc-cso3_e.cfm

www.rcmp.ca

www.uppercanadahistory.ca/finna2.html